What are Florida Kids Saying About Writing Superstars?

"Melissa Forney's new book has everything a kid would ever need for Florida Writes."
Jessie Draper, 5th grade, Port Malabar Elementary

"This book has tons of great ways to improve writing."
Alex Forehand, 4th grade, Lake Mary Elementary

"This book helped me become a better writer! For example, when I got stuck with my writing, I would think about vivid words, transitions, and those awesome color words. I always try to stay away from tacky expressions...now that I know what they are.
Francisco Magro, 4th grade, Alexander Elementary

"At the beginning of my 4th grade year, I was writing 2's, but because of *Writing Superstars,* I have pushed up to 4.5's and 5.0's Since I am the "creativity skills queen" of my classroom, I know I can score a 6.0 on Florida Writes. Roll out the red carpet...here I come!"
Aleyna Villanueva, 4th grade, Grove Park Elementary

"I don't know how I would have accomplished all of the tips if my teacher hadn't shared the books with the class. It has helped me grow from third grade to fourth grade! It's truly superior."
Kendall Jordan, 4th grade, S.S. Dixon Intermediate

"*Writing Superstars* is an awesome way to learn very useful writing skills. I definitely think that *Writing Superstars* is a fantastic book that makes learning much more fun."
Eliza Holtom, 4th grade, Canopy Oaks Elementary

"I enjoyed using the *Writing Superstars* book because the Easy Way to Score helped me get my brain focused on the main idea of what I was writing about. It is one of the most fabulous books ever."
Shereen Rad, 4th grade, Lake Mary Elementary

"*Writing Superstars* has helped me become the 6.0 supersonic writer I am today. The remarkable puzzles, scintillating games, and exquisite samples are quintessential!"
Ryan Thomas, 4th grade, Dodgertown Elementary

"Your *Writing Superstars* book saved my life. Before our class started reading *Writing Superstars,* I hated to write. After reading your book, my writing grades went from 2's and 3's to 4's and 5's!"
Ryan Bell, 4th grade, Sigsbee Elementary

"This quintessential book has model examples of divine million dollar words, supreme examples of scored papers, and fantastic plays! This book has helped me improve my writing skills!"
Jillian McCoy, 4th grade, S.S. Dixon Intermediate

"This book helped me so much. Now my dream is writing kids' books! It's all because of *Writing Superstars!*"
Sarah Gust, 4th grade, Sigsbee Elementary

Writing Superstars

Other Professional Resources by Melissa Forney

Dynamite Writing Ideas
The Writing Menu
Razzle Dazzle Writing
Primary Pizzazz Writing
Melissa Forney's Picture Speller for Young Writers
Melissa Forney's Word Wall Words

Fiction by Melissa Forney

No Regard Beauregard and the Golden Rule
A Medal for Murphy
Oonawassee Summer
To Shape a Life
The Astonishing Journey of Teddy Bodain

Writing Superstars
How to Score More Than Ever Before

Florida Edition

Melissa Forney

WRITING SUPERSTARS
HOW TO SCORE MORE THAN EVER BEFORE
Florida Edition
by Melissa Forney

© 2007 Melissa Jane Forney
All Rights Reserved.

Page design: Melissa Forney
Cover design and art: John Bianchi
Editor: Jareen L. Vichard
Song Lyrics: Melissa Forney
Lyrics for *At Least a Four and Maybe More*: Aaron Odom
Musical Notation for *Bill Grogan's Goat:* PJ Rossi

The idea for Magnetic Panorama, p. 62, is from Mary Doerfler Dall's book,
Little Hands Create (Williamson Books, 2004), and is used with her permission.

The colored alphabet font *Jillustration,* pp. 155 and 164, is used with permission
from www.LetteringDelights.com.

Manufactured in China

Printing No. 10 9 8 7 6 5 4 3 2

Library of Congress Cataloging-in-Publication Data
Forney, Melissa 1952-
        Writing Superstars, How to Score More Than Ever Before, Florida Edition/Melissa Forney.
             p.cm. -- (Writing Superstars)
        Summary: Teaching ideas, hot tips, and results-based strategies
        to help 4th grade students master writing.

ISBN: 978-0-9790094-2-6
Library of Congress Control Number: 2007922724

Published by:

Buttery Moon Multimedia, Inc.

147 N. Industrial Drive
Orange City, FL 32763
Phone: 800-500-8176 or 386-532-3600
Fax: 386-532-3800
www.melissaforney.com

Dedication

To Nancy Prizito and Gretchen Faust,
two superstar teachers who have touched and improved
the lives of hundreds of children, teaching them to love and master writing.

Note to Teachers

Welcome to the world of state mandated writing assessment! While we all feel the pressure of getting 4th grade kids ready for Florida Writes and FCAT Writes+, it doesn't mean that our teaching has to be rigid or dull. Quite the contrary. We have an opportunity to make a difference in the lives of our students, not just for the test, but for the lifetime that stretches ahead of them.

One of the most important things to keep in mind when teaching children how to become writers is that most children are born with a natural penchant toward make-believe, imagination, creativity, the ability to dream and wish, inventiveness, and a healthy dose of curiosity. They thrive in a classroom environment that encourages these activities. Given a safe, encouraging environment, inspiring challenges, models and examples to emulate, plenty of validation, and thought-provoking writing prompts, kids can become eager participants in the writing process. If you keep your writing lessons and test preparation fun and entertaining, you'll have lifelong learners, creative, skillful writers, and students who score to the highest of their abilities on writing assessment tests.

Writing Superstars, How to Score More Than Ever Before, Florida Edition, is designed around 70 writing lessons for fourth grade students. Each lesson focuses on one specific, all-important writing skill. Mastering these skills will empower your kids with confidence, creativity, content, and the ability to write well. Learning these skills will also enable them to score higher than ever before on writing assessment tests.

The lessons are meant to be taught in order. Some lessons are simpler than others and lend themselves to a single daily session. Others are more challenging and might require several days of practice and repetition in order to master them. There is a variety of supplemental materials provided to help your students with repetition and review. They are fun!

In addition to the 70 writing lessons, this book includes information about Florida Writes and FCAT Writes+, patterns for writing manipulatives, games that teach spelling, vocabulary, grammar and punctuation, reference lists, humorous writing songs and plays, all designed to reach even the most reluctant writers.

One of the unique features of *Writing Superstars, How to Score More Than Ever Before, Florida Edition,* is the inclusion of numerous authentic writing samples from Florida students. For the most part, these samples have been reproduced exactly as they were written, without touching up spelling, grammar, or punctuation. The idea is to show kids what other kids their own age are capable of. Although not always perfect, these writing samples serve as resources for ideas, style, technique, scoring, creativity, voice, and supporting with reasons and details. **Writing samples and examples, both long and short, are highlighted in blue so they can easily be identified in your teaching sessions.** Important points to master and remember are highlighted in red. Each writing prompt is featured in a green box.

For your convenience, a full-color printing CD is available for purchase. The printing CD contains 25 full-color graphics pages to make it easier for you to provide high-quality, color manipulatives, games, and medallions for your students. For ordering information, consult page 217 of this book.

Table of Contents

This Book Can Help Your Future! 13

All About Florida Writes 14

Questions About Florida Writes 15

What are the Scorers Looking For? 17

Lesson 1: Thinking of Things to Write 18

    Practice Writing Topics 20

    Writing Skills BINGO 21

Lesson 2: Learning to Work with a Partner 22

Lesson 3: Reading a Prompt 24

Lesson 4: Considering Your Audience 25

Lesson 5: Narrative Clues 26

Lesson 6: Expository Clues 27

Lesson 7: Narrative and Expository Clues. 28

Lesson 8: Brainstorming a Narrative Prompt 29

    Brainstorming Practice 30

Lesson 9: Brainstorming an Expository Prompt 31

    Brainstorming Practice 32

Lesson 10: Beginning, Middle, and Ending 33

    Beginning, Middle, and Ending Sample 35

Lesson 11: Narrative Beginnings 36

    Narrative Beginnings Practice 37

Lesson 12: Expository Beginnings 38

    Expository Beginnings Practice 39

Lesson 13: Writing a Grabber 40

Lesson 14: Types of Grabbers 42

    Grabber Practice 43

Lesson 15: Details in the Middle 44

    Details Writing Sample 45

Lesson 16: Don't Go On and On! 46

Lesson 17: Like-Details Go Together 47

Lesson 18: Conclusions 49

    Conclusion Practice #1 50

    Conclusion Practice #2 51

Lesson 19: Takeaway Endings 52

    Takeaway Ending Practice #1 53

    Takeaway Ending Practice #2 54

    Takeaway Ending Practice #3 55

    Takeaway Ending Writing Sample 56

Florida Writes Format and Organization 57

Terrific Table Tents to Make! 58

Writing Terms Word Search 60

Beginning, Middle, and Ending Paper 61

Lesson 20: Magnetic Panorama 62

Lesson 21: Storyboarding 63

Narrative Storyboard 65

Expository Storyboard 66

Blank Storyboard 67

Narrative Storyboard Questions 68

Expository Storyboard Questions 70

Lesson 22: Temporary Spelling 72

Lesson 23: Jotting 73

Lesson 24: Sentence Variety 74

Lesson 25: Sentence Variety Types 75

Lesson 26: Sentence Combining 76

Sentence Combining Practice 77

Lesson 27: A Feeling of Completeness 78

Lesson 28: Revision 79

Revision Writing Sample 80

Lesson 29: List of Creativity Skills 81

Lesson 30: Style: Puttin' on the "Glitz" 82

Lesson 31: Similes 83

A List of "As" Similes 84

A List of "Like" Similes 84

Lesson 32: Metaphors and Idioms 85

A List of Metaphors and Idioms 86

Lesson 33: Specific Emotion Words and Their Causes 87

Emotion Word Practice 88

Lesson 34: Specific Sensory Words 89

Sensory Word Practice 90

Lesson 35: One-Two Lines of Dialogue 91

Lesson 36: Transitional Phrases 93

Transitional Phrase List 94

Lesson 37: Comparisons 95

Lesson 38: Avoiding Tacky Expressions 96

Lesson 39: Supporting With Reasons and Details 97

Reasons and Details Writing Sample #1 98

Reasons and Details Writing Sample #2 99

Lesson 40: Strong Verbs 100

Strong Verbs Writing Sample 101

A List of Strong Verbs 102

Strong Verbs Crossword 103

Lesson 41: Onomatopoeia 104

Lesson 42: Voice and Passion 105

Voice Writing Sample #1 106

Voice Writing Sample #2 107

Lesson 43: Sizzling Vocabulary 108

Treasure Hunt Vocabulary Game 109

Creativity Slider 110

Lesson 44: Editing 113

Editing Writing Sample 114

Lesson 45: Handwriting 115

Lessons 46-49: Grammar and Punctuation 116

Lesson 50: Seven "Superstar" Punctuation Marks   120
Lesson 51: When to Use Capital Letters   121
Lesson 52: Sentence Fragments   122
          Sentence Fragment Practice   123
Lesson 53: Run-On Sentences   124
Punctuation Practice #1   125
Punctuation Practice #2   126
Punctuation Practice #3   127
Conventions Crossword   128
Survival Skill Game   129
Board Game Questions   132
Race to the Finish Game   141
Lesson 54: Using Your Best Spelling   144
          Dazzling Spelling Word Search   145
          A Spelling List for Genius Writers   146
Lesson 55: Three Parts of Writing You Need to Score Well   153
          "Bulk Up" Your Writing With Weight!   154
Lesson 56: What Does a Narrative Four Look Like?   156
Lesson 57: What Does a Narrative Five Look Like?   157
Lesson 58: What Does a Narrative Six Look Like?   158
Lesson 59: What Does an Expository Four Look Like?   160
Lesson 60: What Does an Expository Five Look Like?   161
Lesson 61: What Does an Expository Six Look Like?   162
Lesson 62: The Easy Way to Score   164
Lesson 63: Scoring Writing Sample #1   166
Lesson 64: Scoring Writing Sample #2   168
Lesson 65: Scoring Writing Sample #3   170
Lesson 66: Scoring Writing Sample #4   172
Lesson 67: Scoring Writing Sample #5   174
          Blank Score Sheet for Young Writers   176
Lesson 68: How to Budget Your 45 Minutes   177
Lesson 69: 6.0 Narrative Writing Sample   178
Lesson 70: 6.0 Expository Writing Sample   180
          Alligator Score Chart   182
          Make Your Own Score Tower   184
          Score Tower   185
Writing Medallions   186
Songs for Genius Writers   188
So You Think You Can Grab   192
Writing Precinct   194
Survivor: Expository Island   197
American Narrative Idol   200
Dr. Zee and the Museum of Ancient Curiosities   204
Paper Bag Writing Folder   208
Answer Keys   210
Bill Grogan's Goat   212
Writing Research   213
Index   215

Acknowledgments

My heartfelt thanks to my personal assistant, Vicki Greening, who keeps me straight, and to Debbie Goguen, who keeps me laughing. I am indebted to Margaret Webb, Jan Rule, Katie Rule, and Rebecca Reynolds for their careful reading of my manuscript. To my daughter and colleague, Rebecca Rossi, I am forever grateful for your support, constructive critiques, and ideas. And, as always, to Rick Forney, collaborator, partner, soul-mate, chauffeur, bodyguard, chef, computer repairman, jack-of-all-trades, husband, and love-of-my-life.

This Book Can Help your Future!

Right now you're probably a kid going to school every day. But before you know it, you'll be grown. That's right. Growing up seems to happen overnight without warning!

When you're an adult, you'll probably want:

something cool to drive!

to own a nice home!

to go out to eat!

YOUR FUTURE

money in the bank!

to take a fancy vacation!

a college degree!

a great job!

YOU CAN HAVE ALL OF THESE THINGS IN THE FUTURE IF YOU PLAN NOW FOR SUCCESS!

One of the most important skills you'll ever learn, a skill that helps you relate to other people, is to express yourself in writing. That's right! Great communication skills lead to many exciting opportunities, including a good job!

This book is going to help you become an incredible writer with more knowledge than most high school students!

All About Florida Writes

Learning how to write well will put you way ahead of most people. Writing doesn't mean handwriting. *Writing* means putting *your thoughts* on paper. You are an amazing kid. You've had lots of experiences. You know things. You have hopes and dreams. You've had funny things happen to you. Write about them.

Good writers have opportunities that non-writers don't have.

Good writers get better grades.

Good writers score high.

Good writers get better jobs.

Good writers communicate well with other people.

As fourth graders, you'll be preparing for Florida Writes, a test that will be given to all fourth graders, usually in February. That may sound like a long way off, but really it's just a few months away.

The GOOD NEWS is: We're going to do this together. As the author of this book, I've created lessons that will help you learn to be terrific writers. Learning to write well can be a great adventure. In the lessons I've prepared, we'll learn one new skill at a time. I've tried to take it step-by-step so things are easy to understand. I've also included games, songs, crafts, plays, and other cool stuff to make learning to write enjoyable. Who says it has to be boring?

Your job is to do your very best. You owe it to yourself to prepare and learn. Soon you'll see that this is a blast. But no slacking! During the months when you and I are preparing, sometimes you'll work alone, sometimes you'll work with a partner, and sometimes you'll work with the whole class. No one likes a goof-off, so keep your head in the game.

Let your parents know what you're learning in school. Show off the skills you master. Bring home some of your papers, and teach your mom and dad the same skills you're learning. Surprise! You might teach them some new skills they've never learned before. Be respectful as you teach, and they'll ask for more and more as you become proficient at writing.

Questions About Florida Writes

Here are some questions and answers about Florida Writes:

1. **Question:** What is Florida Writes?
   Answer: It's a writing exam that tests how well you write.

2. **Question:** When is Florida Writes?
   Answer: Florida Writes is usually the first week in February.

3. **Question:** Where will I take Florida Writes?
   Answer: You'll take it right in your own classroom with your own teacher. Cool!

4. **Question:** Who will score Florida Writes?
   Answer: Ordinary people who have been trained to score will be the scorers.

5. **Question:** Is there a sheet of paper provided for pre-writing?
   Answer: Of course! You also have two sheets to write your rough draft on. You'll also need a couple of sharpened pencils.

6. **Question:** How long will I have to plan and write?
   Answer: You will have 45 minutes.

7. **Question:** What is the test like?
   Answer: You'll be given a booklet. You'll read the writing prompt that is printed in the booklet. You'll think about it, plan your strategy, and then write.

8. **Question:** Will I get a grade for Florida Writes?
   Answer: You will not get a grade. You'll get a score. The highest score is 6.0 and the lowest is a 0. But anyone who follows these lesson plans and worksheets should be able to score at least a 4.0!

9. **Question:** Do I have to score a 6.0 to do well?
   Answer: Our motto is going to be: "At least a four.....maybe more!" A 4.0 is a good score. A 4.5, a 5.0, or a 5.5 is even better. And of course, some kids are such supersonic writers they'll score a 6.0. The good news is you don't have to be a straight "A" student to score a 6.0, and you don't have to be a genius. Ordinary kids can score a 6.0 if they pull out all the stops and show that they know how to write. Ta da!

10. **Question:** How do you get a zero?
    Answer: If you don't write anything, or if you don't write anything on topic, you will get a zero. But come on! Anyone who tries to write on topic should be able to get a higher score than a zero.

11. **Question:** Can I use the posters and notes and writing "helps" in my classroom?
    Answer: No, silly! You'll have all that stuff in your head.

12. **Question:** What is FCAT Writes+?
    Answer: FCAT Writes+ is the second part of the test. It's a multiple choice exam that allows you to show off all the other stuff about writing that you've learned. Don't worry! It's going to be a piece of cake after all the writing lessons we'll do together.

13. **Question:** When will we get the scores back?
    Answer: The scores should be back by the end of the school year.

14. **Question:** Can I get my paper back?
    Answer: Individual papers are not returned.

15. **Question:** How do you get a 6.0?
    Answer: Write an outstanding paper!

16. **Question:** What is the secret to getting a good score?
    Answer: Your paper needs to have a feeling of completeness.
    It needs to have CONTENT and CREATIVITY.
    It needs to have vivid details your reader can picture.
    Don't forget to write with passion!

17. **Question:** What types of prompts will I get?
    Answer: You'll get either an expository prompt, which asks you to explain something, or a narrative prompt, which asks you to tell a story.

18. **Question:** Can my teacher read the prompt aloud?
    Answer: You'll have to read the prompt for yourself. Be sure you read it carefully. Read it two or three times. Then think about it.

19. **Question:** Who has to take Florida Writes?
    Answer: All Florida 4th, 8th, and 10th graders take Florida Writes.

20. **Question:** Why do we have to take Florida Writes and FCAT Writes+?
    Answer: Good question! There are two answers:
    # One: The governor of our state wants to make sure Florida kids are learning the important skills of writing. He wants you to be able to get a good job and do well in life.
    # Two: So you can show off all the really neat stuff you know!

What are the Scorers Looking For?

The official Florida Writes website on the Internet tells us the scorers are looking for four important elements in our writing: Focus, Organization, Support, and Conventions. Here is a chart that can help us understand EXACTLY what they are looking for so we can do our very best.

 FOCUS - Are all of your sentences on the topic? Does every sentence focus on the main idea? Does each paragraph support and develop the main idea?

 ORGANIZATION - Do you have a beginning, a middle, and an ending? Are your ideas in order? Do your thoughts relate to each other? Did you use transitional phrases that take the reader to the "next point?" Does your conclusion tell the reader the main thought you want him to remember?

 SUPPORT - Did you support a main idea with vivid details and juicy descriptions your reader can picture? Did you use sizzling vocabulary words that explain exactly what you mean? Does your writing feel complete?

 CONVENTIONS - Did you start all of your sentences with capital letters and end them with periods? Did you spell most words correctly? Did you sound out and use sizzling words even if you don't Know how to spell them? Did you start some of your sentences differently so they don't all sound the same? Did you use variety in your sentence construction?

Thinking of Things to Write

Some kids are afraid of writing. Don't be scared. Writing is kind of like talking, and talking is pretty easy, if you're interested in the subject.

When you read a writing prompt, stop and think about it. Don't rush. Let your mind picture the subject of the prompt. Use your imagination. Be creative. Think of interesting details you could write about. Consider how you can impress your reader.

When you start to write, try painting a "word picture." Create a "mind movie" that someone else can easily picture and relate to.

Here's an example of a kid who did NOT follow this advice in her writing:

On my birthday I had fun. We did many things. People came over. I got some good stuff. Now tell me about your birthday.

Yikes! Leaping leopards! Has there ever been anything quite so boring? Send this writing to intensive care!

If you were this kid, you'd have to tap into your brainpower.....concentrate on your birthday party....remember who was there....imagine the sights and sounds and activities. Then you'd be ready to write, so your reader can picture your birthday party, almost as if he had been there. Never skimp on the details.

Oooo-eeeee was my birthday an awesome day! We had a house full of company, including my grandparents, my aunties and cousins, and my best friend from school, Delia. My mom and dad and my two little brothers were there, too and, well, you can see there was QUITE a crowd.

Now think some more. You told us WHO was at the birthday party....what else could you tell us about? Aha! Food!

Mom served her world famous hot dogs and mouth-watering chili. My birthday cake was to die for! It was a two-layer chocolate cake with white frosting, "happy birthday," and ten candles.

...Thinking of Things to Write

Don't forget the GAMES!

Since the party was in the back yard, we played a new game called BAGGO. You throw colored bean bags at a target and try to get them into the hole. Delia beat me 12-9.

Keep revving up your brain power! What's a birthday without PRESENTS?

Of course, the best part of having a birthday is the presents! My Auntie Telma bought me a gold necklace that spells my name. Delia gave me two horse books because I love horses and I want to own one someday. But the best gift of all was from my parents. They gave me a new 10-speed bike!

 Read the writing prompt.

 Stop and think about it.

 Don't rush.

 Let your mind picture the subject of the prompt.

 Use your imagination.

 Be creative.

 Think of interesting details you could write about.

 Consider how you can impress your reader.

 When you start to write, try painting a "word picture."

 Create a "mind movie" for your reader.

Practice Writing Topics

Here are some topics you can use for practice writing.

Narrative Topics

A trip to the dentist
Going shopping for something I've wanted
Something scary happened to me
My best friend and I had an adventure
I went to my grandmother's house
I helped cook dinner
I got a new pet
I saw something that made me laugh
I fed the birds in my backyard
My family went to the beach
My family helped someone who needed help
What happened on my birthday
A time I got hurt
I did something that got me into trouble
A time I got lost
Our family faced a big storm
I borrowed something and lost it
My sister told on me
A television show made me laugh
I made a big mistake
I went to the circus/concert/play
I helped clean out and wash the car
My sister and I made brownies
Something woke me up in the night
I made a fort with my friend
I rode my bike somewhere
Someone special came to visit
Something funny made me laugh
I played on the team
We went fishing
Someone hurt my feelings
I acted in a rude way
I had the best day
We went to the mall
We took a trip
I saw something amazing
A dream I've had
A time I made/built something

Expository Topics

My favorite meal
Someone I think is cool
A teacher who rocks
Stuff under my bed
How I get ready for school each morning
What I like to do on a Saturday
Someplace I'd like to visit
An easy-to-make snack
An animal I think is cool
If I could change something about me
Trading "places" with someone for a day
Why hurricanes are dangerous
My grandfather
How our custodian helps our school
The life of a butterfly
How to ride a skateboard
A meal I cooked for my family
A job I'd like to try
Something I'm good at
A real living hero
A magic trick I've learned
Three foods I hate
Stuff I've collected
If I had $200
My favorite present
The people who live with me
Introducing: Our Principal
My church (synagogue, mosque, club, etc.)
Going to the beach is a blast
How to keep from going crazy on a car trip
Something I'm afraid of
How to build a fort
All about my bedroom
A book I enjoyed reading
A chore I do for my family
Bedtime at my house
Something I've learned to do
How to drive my mom nuts

Writing Skills BINGO

"So you'll be familiar with the names of the important writing skills we'll be learning, let's play BINGO with the words. Use the list below to fill in the boxes. Use a random order so your board will be different than anyone else's. As your teacher calls out each skill, put an X through the word. Five in a row in any direction wins!"

style
similes
metaphors
emotion words
sensory words
dialogue
transitional phrases
comparisons

avoid tacky expressions
reasons and details
strong verbs
onomatopoeia
passion
sizzling vocabulary
editing
sentence fragments

punctuation
grammar
readability
left-out words
spelling
run-on sentences
capital letters
scoring

Learning to Work With a Partner

Ah! What a beautiful day. The sun is shining. The birds are singing in the trees. We could be out back in a hammock, walking on a sandy beach, or paddling a canoe down a long, winding river. Here in Florida we've got all kinds of things we could write about: Disney World, the space center, St. Augustine, alligators, birds, Seminole Indians. Jillions of things. It's always a good idea to bounce these ideas off a partner. Two heads are better than one.

Writing is always meant for a reader, even if that reader is yourself.

Writer + Reader = 2

The best writers bounce their ideas off another person. When you are learning to write, it's a good idea to have a partner who can listen and ask questions. A partner can also make suggestions.

Here are a few rules for being a good partner:

Listen With Attention
Compliment Your Partner
Give Encouragement
Answer Questions
Help Each Other
Never Mock or be Unkind

When I attended a special school for writers, I'd never worked with a partner before. I liked writing alone. I didn't want to work with a partner. In class, though, we HAD to work with partners.

Boy, did I learn a lot! When I read my writing to a partner, I got great feedback. She would ask, "What did you mean by *riding in a chiva? What is a chiva?*" or, "Did you hurt yourself when you fell out of the tree?" Her questions made me realize that I had some unanswered questions I needed to answer in my writing. *I* knew what I was talking about, but it was still a mystery for my reader.

Sometimes my partner would laugh at something clever or funny I'd written. That felt great! It made me want to add more funny stuff to my writing.

Other times she would express sorrow, when I wrote about needing to have my little dog put to sleep, or the time when I lost a hundred dollar bill. I realized my writing had power---power to sway someone's feelings!

Best of all, though, my partner would make suggestions.

"Could you add more details about swimming in the waterfall? That's my favorite part. I'd love to do that."

...Learning to Work With a Partner

Or she might say, "Take out these two sentences. They don't really belong here." or, "This sentence is great! But this sentence is kind of boring. Can you change it?"

When my partner made suggestions, I would consider them. Sometimes I saw her point and made a few changes to my writing. Sometimes I preferred to leave it like it was. Sometimes I got good ideas of what other people would be interested in. But I always found that working with a partner helped me grow as a writer.

It's good to work with a partner, especially when you're learning how to write well. Notice the impression your writing makes on your partner. Listen to her specific praise. Consider her suggestions for improving your writing. Ask several other people's opinions so you get different viewpoints.

When you are the listener, show interest. Pay attention. Listen carefully as your partner reads her piece aloud. Compliment the good points. Point out sizzling vocabulary and strong verbs. Show her the most outstanding sentence. Tell her what makes you laugh or what moves you, emotionally. Then, if you can think of any, make good suggestions for improvement. Be gentle! Be encouraging! Be a partner.

When you write for Florida Writes, you will not have the use of a partner. You'll have to work alone. So make use of a partner now while we are in the learning stage.

Autographs of Partners I Have Worked With

Reading a Prompt

Learning the writing skills you've mastered must make you feel proud. Some high school and college kids don't know the things you're learning. Writing will help you get a great job one day in the future.

Today, we're going to look at reading a prompt. Writing prompts are everywhere. Your science book might ask, "Write up the experiment you just did." Or your language arts book could say, "Try writing a different ending to The Three Little Pigs."

But if you're looking at prompts for Florida Writes, they look like this:

narrative

> Everyone has had something funny happen.
> Think of something funny that has happened to you.
> Now tell the story of what happened.

Or,

expository

> Everyone has a chore he doesn't like to do.
> Think of a chore you don't like to do.
> Now explain why you don't like your chore.

Reading a prompt could be confusing if you read it in a big hurry. It's a good idea to read it twice. TWICE, you say? Isn't that a waste of time? Not at all! Part of your Florida Writes score will be determined by how well you answered the prompt. You want to make SURE you've read it carefully, so you can write on topic.

When you read, look for important phrases such as:

chore you don't like to do..... or.....an adventure you have had

Also, look for clue words such as:

explain.....or.....tell the story

The language for writing prompts should always be fairly simple. Prompts are written so kids can understand them. Read carefully, look for important phrases and clue words. Reread the prompt so you are sure what you are being asked to write about.

"ALWAYS BE SURE TO READ THE PROMPT TWICE!"

Considering your Audience

Today we're going to look at your audience. Yes, your audience. Superstars have audiences, but so do writers. You're a writer...so...you have an audience!

The person who reads your writing---the person you are writing for---is your audience. You need to consider who they are, what age they are, and what kind of a relationship you have with them. These things determine the tone of your writing.

If you're writing to your pen-pal, your audience could be another kid your age.

Your tone would be casual, like a kid talking to another kid.

If you're writing a letter to a soldier serving overseas, your audience might be a 22 year old guy or a girl.

Your tone would be friendly but respectful.

If you're writing a thank you letter to your granny, your audience would be a grown lady who is older than your mom.

Your tone would be loving and warm but also respectful.

If you're writing to the President of the United States, your audience is a middle-aged politician.

Your tone would be formal and respectful.

For Florida Writes, your audience will be the person who will read and score your paper. All of the scorers are adults. Since you don't know any of these adults, it might be best to have a light, friendly, upbeat "voice," but also respectful tone. You can be yourself, you can even be charming and humorous, but don't be vulgar, "in your face," or too silly. Put your best foot forward. You will have just one chance to show off your writing skills and style, and you want to showcase your knowledge, talent, and ability to communicate.

Narrative Clues

The writing prompts for Florida Writes are divided into two categories:
narrative and expository.

A narrative means telling a story.

The clue words for narrative prompts are:

> Tell about a time...
> Tell the story...
> Tell about when...

Did you notice that the word "tell" appears over and over? The word "tell" is a clue that you are to write a story. Does it have to be a true story? No! That's one cool thing about being a writer. You can make things up if you want to. You can stretch the truth. You can add details that never happened....all to impress your reader.

Let's pretend that you receive the following narrative prompt:

> Everyone has had an adventure.
> Think about an adventure you have had.
> Now tell about a time you had an adventure.

You might decide to capture your reader's attention right away:

I once was invited to spend a week with Tisha, my Brazilian pen-pal, who lives in Rio de Janeiro, Brazil. My first clue that we were going to have a great adventure together came when her parents picked me up from the airport in a Jaguar convertible.
"Do you like to parachute?" her father asked me.
I swallowed nervously. "I.....uh....don't know..." I stammered. My heart was racing. What had I gotten myself into?

Now, you might never have been to Brazil. You might not even have a Brazilian pen-pal. But when you write to a prompt, you can make things up to entertain your reader. Or, if you want, you can tell a true story:

Last summer my family and I had what we all still call, "The Great Notorious Camping Adventure of 2005." We spent four weeks camping in the mountains of western North Carolina. Little did we know what fun lay ahead...but what obstacles we would have to overcome.

Expository Clues

The word expository means writing to explain something.

The clue words for expository prompts are:

Explain...
In your opinion...
Explain why...

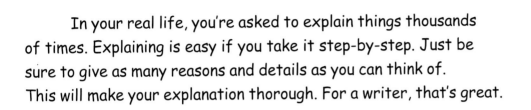

In your real life, you're asked to explain things thousands of times. Explaining is easy if you take it step-by-step. Just be sure to give as many reasons and details as you can think of. This will make your explanation thorough. For a writer, that's great.

Let's imagine you receive the following expository prompt:

> It has been said, "To have a friend you must be a friend." Think of ways to be a good friend. Now explain how to be a good friend.

Remember, an expository prompt asks you to explain. You can't just list friends you have or recall good times. You've got some explaining to do!

Explaining = Important Reasons and Vivid Details

After a short beginning, you'll want to get right into the details that explain what it means to be a good friend. I'll underline the details so you can see what I mean.

You might have all the riches in the world or be the best athlete. But if you aren't a good friend, you're nothing. Being a good friend is one of the most important things in life.

To begin with, a friend is like a treasure you can open when you need it. A friend can be there to <u>comfort you when you're sad</u>. For example, my mom's friend, Caroline, <u>spent two weeks with us</u> when my baby sister died. My mom couldn't stop crying, so <u>Caroline did all the laundry and cooked our meals</u>. She was a friend to our whole family.

Narrative and Expository Clues

"See if you can spot the expository prompts and the narrative prompts.
Put an E in the blank if the prompt is expository.
Put an N in the blank if the prompt is narrative.
Give yourself 2 points for every one you get right!"

1. _____ Explain why kids should be given an allowance.

2. _____ What is your favorite restaurant, and why is it your favorite?

3. _____ Tell about a time when you did something nice for someone else.

4. _____ Explain how to make your favorite after-school snack.

5. _____ Tell about a time when something embarrassing happened to you.

6. _____ In your opinion, what circus animal would make the best pet?

7. _____ The principal calls you to the office and points you to a limo outside. As you approach the limo, the window slowly rolls down. Tell the story of what happens next.

8. _____ Convince us that kids should not have to go to school in the summer.

9. _____ You find an unusual book in a trunk in your grandmother's attic. It is a storybook for kids. When you open the pages, the characters in the pictures come alive and invite you into the story. What happens next?

10. _____ Explain what is involved in taking care of a dog.

11. _____ You are visiting the circus. You hear shouting and see zookeepers running everywhere. Someone has accidentally left open the chimpanzee cage! Tell the story of what happens and how you save the day.

12. _____ Every kid has a dream of what he'd like to be when he grows up. Think of what you'd like to be when you grow up. Now explain what you'd like to be.

13. _____ Think about a time when something scary happened to you. Now tell the story.

14. _____ Think of a person who has helped shape your life. Now explain why this person has shaped your life.

Score: 1-10   points = You're taking baby steps!
         11-18   points = You might win a turtle race!
         19-25   points = Skipping right along there!
         26-28 points = You've crossed the finish line!!!

Brainstorming a Narrative Prompt

You've already learned about narrative and expository prompts and their clue words. Now we're going to look at brainstorming. Isn't that a funny word, brainstorming?

Brainstorming means to think quickly and creatively.

Once you've read the prompt, it's time to brainstorm ideas. Make a mental list of ideas that pop into your head that might go with the prompt. You can even make a quick list of these ideas.

For instance, if the prompt asks you to tell about a time when you had an accident, you know it's asking you to *tell a story*. You could then make a list of details that come to mind about a story that's happened to you. The story could be true or one you make up.

Mom said not to jump on the bed
I climbed on the top bunk
started jumping with Paul
laughed like a maniac
fell off !!!
hit the railing
bounced off
broke my arm and my toe
broken arm looked SICK!
hurt like crazy
cast & splint
learned my lesson

If the prompt asks you to tell about a great day you've had, and you instantly remember the day you competed in a horse show, think of the highlights that would be interesting for your reader:

Winnie and I had practiced jumping for months
I got up early to bathe and groom Winnie
Drove to the show
We sailed over every jump – no "ticks"
Won first place
Got a blue ribbon
Had our picture taken with Tobey Maguire!

Brainstorming Practice

See how many details you can brainstorm from the following narrative prompt:

> Everyone has broken something before.
> Think of something you have broken.
> Now tell about a time when you broke something.

You don't have to actually write the prompt. Just brainstorm as many details as you can remember. If you can't remember a time when you broke something, make one up and brainstorm imaginary details. List as many as you can:

_____

_____

_____

_____

_____

_____

_____

_____

_____

_____

_____

Did you think of lots of details? Good for you! Compare your details with those written by some of the kids in your class. Help each other improve.

Brainstorming an Expository Prompt

We've learned that an expository prompt asks you to **explain**. Read the following prompt. Now read it again to make sure you understand what the prompt is asking you to do.

> Everyone has favorite things he or she likes to do on the weekend. Think of some things you like to do. Now explain what you like to do on the weekend.

Now that you've read the prompt twice, let's review how to brainstorm ideas for an expository prompt. First, we think. Concentrate on the weekend. Picture things you like to do for fun. Think about places your family goes on the weekend....where....why....who is with you...those kinds of details. As we think, we would make a list of important words. You might not end up writing about ALL of them, but at least you'll have a good list to choose from:

eat pizza	help with our garage sale
have a friend over	go swimming
rent a movie	go to church
make popcorn	eat my mom's dinner
stay up late	jump my bike
sleep late	play with my dog

Now that's a pretty good list! If you were asked to write about the weekend, you'd have excellent choices of details.

If an expository prompt asks us to **explain why it's not wise to smoke,** we would go through the same brainstorming process. Think about the topic, concentrate on details and reasons that would help you explain the prompt:

cancer	tobacco is expensive
lung diseases	babies have to breathe it
smoke stinks	smoke damages things
heart damage	your body can't heal
other people	smoking is addictive

This list was a little harder to come up with than the list about the weekend. I was worried for a second or two. But with some thought and concentration, I came up with good reasons and details to explain why smoking is not wise.

Brainstorming Practice

By now, you know that brainstorming can be done by yourself or with a group of other writers. It's simply concentrating on a topic and thinking of all the details you COULD write about. Read the following expository prompt.

> We learn many things in school.
> Think of some things you have learned in school.
> Now explain some things you have learned in school.

Brainstorm as many details as you can think of that you could write about.
Remember to be specific. In other words, don't just list the subjects you study each day. Think about specific skills and knowledge you have actually *learned*, and list those here:

_____

_____

_____

_____   _____

_____   _____

_____   _____

_____   _____

_____   _____

_____   _____

Take turns reading your details aloud. Listen and learn from each other.

Beginning, Middle, and Ending

It doesn't matter if you're writing a piece that is three sentences long, one paragraph long, or five or six paragraphs long. Writing should be divided into three parts:

beginning middle ending

BEGINNING

The beginning should be short and to the point. Immediately let your reader know what your topic is. In a narrative piece, the beginning lets the reader know that you are going to tell a story. In an expository piece, the beginning makes an important statement that can be explained and supported with reasons and details.

MIDDLE

The middle of both narrative and expository pieces should be filled with juicy details, examples, quotes, comparisons, personal experiences, mini-stories, or reasons.

ENDING

The ending should be short. Close your piece by telling your reader the most important point you want her to remember. Read this short, expository sample.

Expository Prompt: Write a short piece about your best friend.

Veronica has long brown hair. Her eyes are blue like mine. She lives next door. We play sometimes and climb trees. I like Veronica a lot. I guess she's my best friend. Her skin is a little browner than mine and she has freckles. Do you like freckles? I do. I wish I had freckles. She and I like to sing together and put on plays. I sing good. Oh, her last name is Vasquez. My last name is Williams.

The writer needs a beginning! There is no sentence that tells us this piece is going to be about her friend and next-door neighbor.

The writer needs a middle! If she's going to write about Veronica, she must let us know more details about her---ones that we will be interested in. It's doubtful that many people will even care if someone likes freckles. Describing someone so your reader can picture what she looks like is not as important as telling how you met, what you do together, where you've been together, and some adventures.

The writer needs an ending! The piece just stops. Yikes!

...Beginning, Middle, Ending

Now this piece is a big improvement over the last attempt. We can see that it has a clear beginning, a middle, and an ending:

beginning

I'm so lucky to have a best friend who is also my next door neighbor.

middle

Veronica Vasquez and I met when we were three years old. We've been playing together ever since. Hardly a day goes by that we don't climb the big oak tree that grows between our houses. From way up there, we spy on the boys and listen in as our moms talk in the back yard. Sometimes we play funny tricks on them. Veronica and I ride bikes all over the whole neighborhood, especially down to the 7-11, where we buy snacks and sodas.

Sometimes we spend the night at each other's houses, and that's where the craziness begins! Once, we dressed up in costumes and made a video. It was hilarious! My family and Veronica's family usually have a barbecue in the back yard about once a month. Friends come over, too. Veronica and I perform our songs and plays as the entertainment. We are the stars!

ending

Veronica and I have so much fun together, and we get along super. I bet we'll be friends for the rest of our lives.

The **beginning** is short, to the point, and lets the reader know that the author is writing about her best friend.

The **middle** includes details about when the girls met, what they do for fun, where they do it, and why. Each of these details supports the main idea. The middle also includes a mini-story. Did you spot it? The clue word is "Once."

The **ending** tells the reader the most important thought.

Could this piece be longer? Oh yes! This piece could be developed and stretched into two to three more paragraphs. Several of the sentences in the middle could be developed by adding more details. For instance, the reader would love to know what kind of tricks were played, how the boys reacted to being tricked, and what happened as a result.

Beginning, Middle, and Ending Sample

I think you'll enjoy this writing sample from a Florida 4th grade girl. After you read it for enjoyment, go back and find the beginning, middle and the ending.

Narrative Prompt: Write a narrative story about a magic carpet ride.

"Susan! There's a package for you!" my mother called from the kitchen. I ran down the stairs and seized the package. My pen-pal from China sent the strangest things, and I loved them.

I tore the brown wrapping paper as excited as a person going on The Incredible Hulk roller coaster at Universal Studios. But after all the pink tissue paper was gone, my excitement faded. All that was in the package was a dusty old rug. I could tell once it had been grand because there were golden frills around it, now much splotched and the purple color faded. The panda picture in the middle though, glowed. I then noticed a note. It read: "Dear Pen-pal, This is a magic carpet. Just tap the panda twice, and yell where you want to go."

Without a second thought, I jumped on the carpet and yelled out the word "Alaska." Whoosh! We were off!

Brrr...only then did I realize that I should've brought a coat. But winter in Florida was only the slightest bit chilly, so how was I to know? I looked around and saw a pair of amber eyes. They stared at me, and then out came gray fur and four legs. It was a wolf! I started to scramble away, but the wolf was fast. It was gaining on me! All of a sudden, there were no pads behind me. I turned to see a gray streak after a cute little snow hare. I breathed a sigh of relief.

I picked up the carpet and rolled it up and began wandering around. The woods were silent, and Alaska was beginning to get dull. Just as I was unrolling the carpet, I fell through the snow and landed in a hole. It was too icy to climb out of, so I began shouting for help. Wait! I had a magic carpet! I quickly unrolled the carpet, tapped the panda two times, and shouted, "Home, home, HOME!!!" In a split second we were going at full speed.

Thump! I was back in my room, my magic carpet was next to me. I smiled at the carpet. Boy, was that a great adventure. I have been to many places with my carpet now. My pen-pal sent me lots more things but as weeks flew by, they were neglected. But my magic carpet never was and never will be.

Narrative Beginnings

¡Hola! ¿Comó estás? Vamos a escribir.

Hello! How are you? Let's write.

When it comes to writing stories, remember this important point:

A narrative beginning should be short and to the point.

A narrative beginning lets the reader know you are going to tell a story.

Here are four examples of **narrative beginnings** for you to see:

1. Last summer at my Uncle Carl's, I had the <u>adventure of my life</u>.
2. The time I <u>accidentally spilled black ink</u> on my mom's favorite sofa is <u>a day that will live in my memory forever</u>.
3. <u>Secretly wearing your sister's new blouse is never a good idea</u>,
4. When I wandered into the woods behind my house, I <u>didn't mean to get lost for two days</u>, really I didn't.

Notice how each of these sentences gets right to the point. They don't dilly-dally here and there. They don't go on and on. They tell you right away what the subject is. Each of these sentences "promises" a story.

A reader might read these beginning sentences and ask himself:

1. What happened at Uncle Carl's? What kind of adventure did you have?
2. How did you spill ink on the sofa? What did your mom do?
3. It sounds like something bad happened when you wore your sister's new blouse without her knowing. Did you ruin it in some way?
4. Yikes! You got lost in the woods? For two days? How did you survive? You ran into a hedgehog? We're waiting to hear the story!

So when you get ready to write a beginning for a narrative piece, remember to get right to the point. Try to tell your reader what the piece is going to be about without giving away too many details. Save those juicy details for the middle of your piece.

Narrative Beginnings Practice

"Now, it's your turn. Here are some narrative subjects. It's time for you to practice writing narrative beginnings that are short and to the point. Remember to write a sentence that "promises" a story. The beginning can be true or....one you make up."

1. Something embarrassing happened to you.

_____

_____

2. You did something to make your parents proud.

_____

_____

3. Something scary happened to you.

_____

_____

4. You went on a vacation.

_____

_____

5. You won an award.

_____

_____

Take turns reading your narrative beginnings aloud. Compliment each other on great beginnings. Help your fellow writers improve. Be open for suggestions.

Expository Beginnings

Let's start at the very beginning. A very good place to start! When you read, you begin with A,B,C. When you sing, you begin with do-re-mi. Do-re-mi.

And when you start an expository piece, you need an expository beginning!

In expository writing:

The beginning should be short and to the point.
The beginning should introduce the subject.
The beginning should be a statement that can be explained.

Here are four examples of **expository beginnings** I've written for you:

1. Max Creedle is the <u>best friend</u> any kid could have.
2. Hingle Elementary is <u>not my favorite place to go to school</u>.
3. Taking care of elephants at the zoo is the <u>coolest job</u> in the world.
4. Believe me, <u>you're lucky you don't have to live with my six-year-old twin brothers, Tyler and Tyson</u>.

Each of these beginning sentences introduces a subject and says something about it that will have to be explained. That's why these are **expository beginnings**. I've underlined the key words and phrases that will have to be explained later in the middle of the writing piece.

A reader might read these beginning sentences and ask himself:

1. Who is Max Creedle? What makes him such a good friend?
2. What is it about Hingle Elementary that you do not like?
3. What is cool about taking care of elephants?
4. What's so bad about those little twin brothers?

An expository beginning has to get right to the point of what you're writing about. It should also be a statement that needs to be explained with reasons and details.

Expository Beginnings Practice

"What's up, Dawg? I'll give you an expository subject. You practice writing a beginning that gets right to the point. Remember to write a statement that could be explained later with reasons and details, okay? Use your imagination and make things up if you want to."

1. A Field Trip

_____

_____

2. Cleaning the Kitchen

_____

_____

3. Your Favorite Book

_____

_____

4. Music Class

_____

_____

5. Kids and Pets

_____

_____

Take turns reading your expository beginnings aloud. Notice which ones sizzle and which ones fizzle. Learn from other good writers in your class. Help each other improve.

Writing a Grabber

You've already learned beginnings...so...what's a grabber? Isn't a grabber part of the beginning? Isn't a grabber the very first thing you write?

Well, yes. I've been keeping that a secret. I wanted you to first learn how to write a *beginning* that is short, to the point, and tells the reader what you're writing about. Now, for you really brilliant kids, it's time to tackle *grabbers*.

A grabber is an opening sentence that
immediately captures the reader's attention.

Okay, we got that straight. Now let's learn to write one.

Let's say the P.E. coach at your school is a really cool guy, and everybody at school thinks he rocks. You're going to write an expository piece about him, explaining what makes him so much fun. The beginning of your piece must be short, to the point, and introduce the topic. So here's your beginning:

Coach Mathison is the world's champion P.E. coach, hands down.

Terrific beginning. We know you're writing about your coach. We know you think he's terrific. We're ready for you to explain why you think he's the best. So, what would a great grabber look like?

A grabber comes before the actual beginning sentence and is a "teaser" that pulls the reader into the piece, making him want to read more:

He's bald, he's huge, but he's the best thing that ever happened to Jefferson Elementary School. Coach Mathison is the world's champion P.E. coach, hands down.

When you read "He's bald, he's huge, but he's the best thing that ever happened to Jefferson Elementary School," you wonder: Who is bald and huge? What makes him the best thing that happened to this school?

After the grabber and the beginning, your challenge as a writer would be to explain all the qualities and actions that make Coach Mathison a great coach and P.E. teacher.

...Writing a Grabber

Let's try some more, just to be sure you understand grabbers. Imagine you are asked to write a piece on a profession you'd like to try when you grow up. Your beginning is:

I think being a dolphin trainer would be an incredible, adventuresome job.

We know this is the beginning of your piece because it's short, to the point, and tells the reader what your subject is. After you write the beginning sentence, you choose to go back up above the sentence you just wrote and write a grabber:

<u>You swim and communicate with one of nature's smartest mammals. The two of you form a bond that will last a lifetime.</u> *I think being a dolphin trainer would be a fantastic profession.*

The two sentences that were just added **before** the beginning form the grabber. They add just enough mystery to capture the reader's attention.

Here's another example. See if you can underline the grabber. Circle the beginning sentence that tells the reader what the subject is:

"That will be $2.99, please." She hands me a tall styrofoam cup mounded up with the coldest, creamiest, most delicious treat a kid could ever imagine. Oh, how I love a real, New Orleans-style snowball! You just can't imagine how scrumptious it is.

Doesn't that grabber make you want to read more? After reading the beginning, I bet you want to try one, too. Here's one more example of a grabber, and it's a little longer than usual. Underline the grabber. Circle the beginning sentence that tells the reader what the subject is:

Her poison is one of the deadliest on Earth. Her fangs can strike at the speed of light. She waits on the walking path for prey to come by. The fer-de-lance is one snake you want to avoid at all costs!

Types of Grabbers

Keep this list of grabber types handy. Each one captures the reader's attention.

Scenario

Picture this: Your two-year-old sister pours spaghetti in her hair. She draws on the bathroom wall with a permanent marker and eats dog food when your back is turned. Now imagine your mom complaining, "Were you watching your sister, or not?" Baby-sitting is not an easy job, let me tell you.

Voice

Man, it bugs me and it bugs me bad. Our teacher gives at least two hours of homework every night. Two hours of homework is entirely TOO MUCH!

Mystery

"Eeeeeeeeaaaaaaooooow...." The eerie moaning woke me from a deep sleep. I had no idea what was making that sound, but I was going to find out. While my grandmother slept soundly, I decided to investigate what I now call...the attic of DOOM.

Opinion

It's hot, it's cheesy, and I could eat it till I bust. Pizza Hut's new Full House XL Pizza is melt-in-your-mouth delicious.

Onomatopoeia

Vroom! Vroom! A cloud of dust billows up around us. Neighbors stare. So starts our father-son getaway in my dad's restored hot rod. It's a trip I will remember for the rest of my life.

Dialogue

"Jody, get these clothes picked up or you're not going anywhere," my mother screams. It's time for the dreaded chore: cleaning my room.

Global statement/Specific statement

Every kid should be lucky enough to go to a good school. I'm fortunate to go to South Port Elementary School, one of the best schools around.

Rhetorical Question

Have you ever been so scared that you almost jumped out of your skin?

Funny Statement

I'd rather be abducted by fuzzy-haired, purple people eaters than have to take the garbage out every night.

Grabber Practice

"Okay, genius writers, read the beginning sentences below. Then write a grabber sentence that would come before the beginning sentence and capture the reader's attention."

1. _____

_____

_____

_____

Steve Irwin, The Crocodile Hunter, was my hero.

2. _____

_____

_____

_____

New clothes cost too much money.

3. _____

_____

_____

I still cringe when I think of the time I dropped my tray in the cafeteria in front of everyone!

Details in the Middle:
Creating "Mind Movies" for your Reader

Five, four, three, two, one, BLAST OFF!!!!

It's time to master another writing lesson that will add pizzazz to your writing. Let's look at what we need in the middle of our pieces to make them absolutely supersonic.

The middle, also known as the *body* of our writing, is where all the details live. The middle of our writing is the main event, the featured attraction, the BIG BANANA!

When we write details in the middle, we should keep in mind creating "mind movies" for our reader. What is a "mind movie," you ask? Well, think about it. In our minds, we have movie projectors that show images and memories in vivid details.

When you think of an experience you've had...say...riding the ShieKra at Busch Gardens--you immediately recall the rail in front of you, the whoosh of speed, and the spray of water as you whiz over the lagoon. You hear yourself and your friends laughing and screaming. You picture these things in your mind's eye as a "mind movie," almost like a real movie, only better.

Now, when you write about riding the ShieKra, you've got to create "mind movies" for your reader. That means including all of the juicy details that made it an awesome, scare-you-to-death experience.

Whether you're explaining information or telling a story, try to use all of the five senses to describe, so your reader will be able to use his imagination. After a fantastic grabber and beginning sentence, move on to the middle to give details like these:

I try to leave my hands raised in the air to show off how brave I am. But as soon as we come to the first drop-off, and it looks as if we are going to free-fall, I scream like a little baby and grip the bar in front of me with both hands, digging my nails in deep. Huge rooster tails of water goosh sky high when our car whizzes over the water lagoon below. The white, watery mist covers us from head to toe, soaking us as we pass at lightning speed. ShieKra then lurches around a corner, going at least 60 miles per hour, and my stomach feels like it's being ripped out of my body by a giant arm.

Now, that's a "mind movie" if I ever read one!

Details Writing Sample

Here's an **expository** writing sample from a 5th grade girl. She writes details we can picture, details that help us form "mind movies" in our imaginations.

Expository prompt: Write an expository piece about your favorite possession.

My most prized possession is hidden in a secret place in my room that only I know about. It is a Chinese dime.

I found it in my room when I was only three years old. I was climbing on a bar in my closet that I use to hang my jackets and sweaters on. One day, I slipped off the bar and plunged deep into the box that I keep my books in. Books flew in every direction. I dove out of the box and began tossing the books back into it. I lifted a book off the ground and uncovered a shiny, gold coin. It was smaller than a nickel but bigger than a penny. It had Chinese writing on it and the number 10. I dashed down the hall and scanned the kitchen for my mom. I spotted her and skid to a halt right before I crashed into her.

"Mom, Mom! What kind of penny is this?" I asked her eagerly.

"It's not a penny," she replied. "It's a Chinese dime. Where did you get it?"

"I found it in my room," I explained. "I'm going to start collecting money from different countries!"

That Chinese dime is now with my incomplete collection of foreign money.

With a better ending, there's no reason this paper couldn't get a score of 6.0. The writer took special care to fill the middle with vivid, picturesque details that are easy for us, her readers, to imagine.

Don't Go On and On!

Good writing should be entertaining, yet not skimpy. The trick is to write all the good stuff you can and leave out details that are boring or unnecessary. Don't go on and on just to fill up the paper. Some kids write bunches of stuff, and it's either boring or it doesn't make much sense. Or worse, they get off topic. Never get off topic. I mean, NEVER!!!!

This paragraph is filled with unnecessary details:

My best friend's name is Jamie. We went to a BMX bike race yesterday. My mom drove us there in her car. On the way we bought a smoothie. I finished my smoothie before we got there but Jamie didn't. The BMX stadium is an hour away from our house. We talked on the way and told corny jokes. I know some good ones. We finally got there at 1:45.

Lots of readers would want to read about a BMX bike race. But how you got there or what you drank along the way are boring details. Who cares if the stadium is an hour away from your house or what time you got there? Even the name of your best friend might not matter to a reader unless Jamie is an important part of the story.

Instead, you could say the same thing in much less time:

My best friend and I went to a BMX bike race yesterday. Wow! We had one INCREDIBLE day!

Simplifying this section of your writing allows you to get to the juicy part: the middle. Save most of your time for writing vivid details in the middle of your writing, details which will be entertaining for your reader.

Here's another example of a writer who goes on and on and gets off topic:

Do you want me to tell you a story? Okay, here goes. Last summer I went water skiing with my Uncle Mark. He's my mom's brother. He does lots of things with us. Oh, I forgot to tell you. Mark is 6 feet 6 inches tall. Whoa!!!! That's tall!!!! Anyway, back to my story. See, we went water skiing in a lake up in Georgia. We can't water ski here in Florida because there are gators in all of the lakes and my mom freaks out.

I underlined the phrases and sentences that are important. The rest is fluff!

Like-Details Go Together

When it comes to supporting our writing with details and reasons, it's good to group things so they go together. That way your reader can concentrate on one idea at a time.

Think about a house. The pots, pans, dishes, and glasses are in the kitchen so you can reach the things you need to cook and eat. Shampoo, soap, toothpaste, and toothbrush are grouped together in the bathroom where they'll be handy. Your bedroom has a bed, a dresser, and a closet because you use those things when you're sleeping or dressing. Things in a house are grouped to go together, right?

Writing should be the same. We group things together so they'll make sense.

This young author, writing an expository piece about his pet pig, has details that are all mixed-up. That makes the writing confusing and disorderly:

Taking care of Baby, my potbellied pig, isn't easy. I have to give Baby a bath once a week or he stinks. First I tie Baby up to the railing on our back porch. He loves taking a bath, but not nearly as much as he likes to eat. I feed him twice a day. In the morning he gets Purina pig chow. In the evening I give him all the scraps from our dinner and whatever leftovers my mom has. Next I get a big plastic tub and fill it with our garden hose. Baby loves stale cookies! I wet him down and scrub him with baby shampoo and a plastic brush. You should see Baby when he's being scrubbed. He rolls on his back and moans and kicks his legs because it feels so good. His favorite food is ice cream. He moans when he gets ice cream, too. And you should see how clean I can get his ears!

Good grief! Are we talking about giving Baby a bath or feeding him? The details are all higgledy-piggledy (I couldn't help that pun). It's better to keep like-things together because the writing makes more sense to the reader.

When you pre-write, and plan the details that will go in the middle of your writing, try to group them so like-things are together.

...Like-Details

Let's pretend the writer rewrote his piece so that it makes more sense. Kids with sharp eyes will notice that this time, the details go together:

Taking care of Baby, my potbellied pig, isn't easy. I have to give Baby a bath once a week so he won't stink. The first step is to tie Baby up to the railing on our back porch. This isn't too much trouble, even though he weighs 52 pounds, because Baby loves taking a bath. Next, I get a big plastic tub and fill it with our garden hose. After I fill the tub, I wet Baby down and scrub him with baby shampoo and a plastic brush. You should see him when he's being scrubbed! He rolls on his back and moans and kicks his legs with pleasure. This is so funny that some of the neighborhood kids come over to watch. When Baby has been scrubbed all over and is as clean as a potbellied pig can be, I towel him dry from head to toe. Now this is the hard part. Baby feels so clean and frisky he wants to run free all around the back yard. He tugs and grunts and pulls against the rope like the crazy pig that he is. Once, he even knocked me into the tub. But in the end, after a lot of toweling and rubbing, he's dry and I can let him off the rope. Bathing Baby is my once-a-week chore, but afterwards he is one clean, happy pig.

This time the author focused on one thing at a time and kept like-details together. He could now write other paragraphs about feeding Baby, playing with Baby, and so on, until the middle of his piece feels complete.

The author also used transitional words and phrases, which lead the reader to keep on reading. Find and circle the transitional phrases listed below in the paragraph above.

The first step...   Now this is the hard part...
Next...   Once...
After I fill the tub...   But in the end...
When Baby has been scrubbed all over...   but afterwards...

Conclusions

We've looked at beginnings, middles, and now, we've arrived at endings. As you can imagine, every writing piece needs an ending.

An ending that tells the reader the most important thought you want him to remember is called a conclusion.

Let's look at the word "conclusion." Say it. Con-clu-sion. It sounds like it has the word "clue" in it. A detective looks for clues. When he examines the clues he has found, they usually lead him to form some sort of a conclusion, good or bad.

The dictionary tells us:

A conclusion is a decision based on facts.

If a detective summoned to someone's home comes across a broken window, a jimmied door lock, muddy footprints that lead into the house, evidence that a television set and a computer have been stolen, footprints leading out of the house, and the back door standing open, these are each **clues**. When he examines the clues, they lead him to a **conclusion**. In this case, the conclusion would be that the house has been broken into by a thief.

When you finish writing your beginning and middle, you should be able to look back through your writing and see key points, or **clues**. These clues should then lead you to a conclusion. The conclusion is the most important thing you want to say about something.

So if you're writing about your class field trip to Sea World, when you get to the end of your piece, look back through the middle of your piece for clues. If you wrote these key words and phrases,

dolphins can communicate with their trainers
young dolphin males swim in packs
manatee mothers produce rich, rich milk for their calves
manatees can live as long as humans
full-grown killer whales are 32 feet long
macaws can be trained to do amazing tricks
African gray parrots can be taught to say over 300 words

you could look back at these "clues" and come up with a conclusion such as the following:

My trip to Sea World taught me many fascinating facts about animals and reminded me why I am planning to become an animal trainer when I grow up.

Conclusion Practice #1

Read the following short passages. Look for clues as you read. Write a conclusion based on those clues. Be sure to tell the reader the most important thought you want her to remember.

narrative

Fireworks

Last summer my cousin Thaddeus used all of his savings to buy fireworks for our family's big 4th of July celebration.

The fireworks were beautiful, but I was nervous the entire time he was shooting them off. For one thing, he didn't use a long punk stick to light them with. He used matches. When they went off, they were very close to his hand and fingers. Instead of putting the bottle rockets in glass bottles to shoot them off, he just stuck them in the ground. Some of them went off all crazy-like and shot out through the crowd. But the worst part was when he shot off a parachute rocket. It caught the fabric on fire and came down on top of my dad's new Ford Expedition.

_____

_____

expository

Dishes!

Wouldn't you know it? The most dreaded chore of all times is mine! Whenever my sister cooks dinner for our family, my mom makes ME do all of the dishes.

My sister never cleans up as she goes. Oh no, not Candace! She drops things on the floor and even steps on them and squashes them when she's walking around the kitchen. Sometimes the pots and pans are burned and stuff is stuck on them and in them an inch thick. If we have something like rice, she never remembers to fill the empty pot with water. I have to spend 30 minutes scrubbing and scraping out stuck rice until my muscles are as big as a Russian weight lifter's. But the most terrible thing of all is that she uses every pot, pan, plate, and bowl we own, so it takes me more than an hour of work before my mom will let me out of there!!!!

_____

_____

Take turns writing your conclusions on the board. Celebrate all good conclusions!

Conclusion Practice #2

Read the following short passages. Look for clues as you read. Write a conclusion based on those clues. Be sure to tell the reader the most important thought.

Shoes

narrative

"I'm not buying those shoes for you," my dad said. "They're much too expensive. Besides, you're growing like a weed. You won't get enough wear out of them." That's what my dad told me when I begged for a new pair of tennis shoes last May. What did he know? I wanted those shoes!

I pleaded. I jumped up and down. I practically howled at the moon. Finally Dad agreed to lend me the money. A huge grin spread across my face. I promised to pay him back and walked out of the store wearing the best shoes in the universe. I forgot how long it would take me to earn $115!

I had to mow yards all summer and wash windows to get the money to pay Dad back. I'm talking, every day! I wore old ugly tennis shoes with holes in them so I wouldn't ruin my new ones while I worked. I had to work in the hot sun. When my friends went to the beach I still had to work. I gave Dad the last of the money on July 29. I felt free!

I wore my shoes for two glorious weeks. My friends thought they were the ultimate cool. Then, one day I went to put on my shoes and noticed that they were too small! Ackkkk!

_____

_____

Kites

expository

They soar and glide. Their colors burst across the sky. Flying a kite makes me happier than you can imagine!

I make my kites myself out of paper, balsa wood strips, kite string, and strips of cloth. I paint the paper brilliant colors like lemon, pink, pistachio, tangerine, and purple. I use wood glue to hold the paper to the frame. One fun part is making the tail. I cut the strips from beautiful cloth my mom saves for me from her quilt-making.

But the best part is flying the kite. On a windy day (but not too windy!), I gather loose string in one hand and start running with my kite. I release the kite to the wind and let out string.

_____

_____

Takeaway Endings

...I learned a valuable lesson the day I accidentally set the kitchen on fire: never cook on the stove when my mom and dad aren't home. I'll be more careful next time, believe me, because I don't want to destroy the place where we live and I want to live a long, long time!

And that, ladies and gentlemen, is what a takeaway ending looks like!

An ending that tells the reader the lesson you learned or how your life changed is called a takeaway ending.

...I don't think I'll ever look at an ostrich again and not think of the day I let my sister talk me into participating in the ostrich race.

A "takeaway" is a nugget of truth we learn from life's experiences. Sometimes that truth is so great that it changes our lives or the way we look at things forever. We find takeaways at the end of movies, books, stories, soap operas, and plays. Be on the lookout for takeaway endings!

"Crime doesn't pay," I said, wishing I had never lied to my mother about breaking her favorite lamp. "I'll be more careful next time."

After spending three weeks grounded without any friends or television, I don't think I'll disobey my dad ever again.

The summer my brother and I helped build the barn together proved to us that we are not only brothers, but best friends.

The next time I'm tempted to sneak out at night, I'll remember the trouble we got into and jump right back in my bed!

There are many ways to write takeaways, but here are some key words:

The lesson I learned...	I'll always remember...	Learn from my example...
I learned a valuable lesson...	You can be sure that...	I realized that...
For the rest of my life...	The next time...	...has changed my life
From that day on...	Be careful when...	Now I know...

Takeaway Ending Practice #1

Read the following **narrative** piece. Write a takeaway ending based on what this writer might have learned or how you think her life has changed as a result of this story.

Narrative Prompt: Write about a time you got in trouble.

BUSTED!

Have you ever done something you instantly regretted? I still have nightmares about the time I got into my sister's stuff and she had a total MELTDOWN!

Last Thursday when my sister, Regina, went to middle school, I stayed home from school sick. I wasn't that sick and after a while I got bored. I entertained myself by snooping around in Regina's room. She hates for me to go in there so my mom has told me that Regina's room is "off limits." But my mom had to go to the grocery store for a little while and she left me home alone.

First, I messed around in Regina's makeup. She's got some cool makeup, and I put on some of everything she has. Then I tried on her jewelry. Regina makes her own jewelry so she's got all sorts of colorful necklaces, bracelets, and earrings. I put on a turquoise blue set, and it looked great with the makeup.

I remembered that Regina had recently bought a new blouse that I wanted to try on. In no time, I found it in her closet. Of course, then I needed a skirt to go with it, so I found one of her new ones, too.

I put on the stereo and started dancing. Man, did I think I looked good in her makeup and jewelry and clothes. I was jumping around all over the room, singing to the stereo, when I heard my mom's voice coming up the stairs!

"Heather, where are you, honey?" my mom called. "Are you okay?"

As fast as you can even imagine I tore off my sister's clothes. I ripped that jewelry off and threw it in a drawer. Just as my mom neared the top of the stairs I dashed across the hall and jumped in bed, wiping the makeup off my face with my sheet!

"I'm fine," I said as my mom came in the room to check me. She believed me! I thought I was safe. I forgot all about my little spy-trip into my sister's room.

But that night my sister was supposed to go to a basketball game with her friends. After dinner she raced upstairs to change into...her new blouse and skirt.

"MOM!!!!!" Regina's voice could be heard all the way to China! I knew I was in big trouble. It seems that when I whipped her blouse up over my head I had smeared makeup all over the front of it.

_____

_____

_____

Takeaway Ending Practice #2

Read the following **narrative** piece. Write a takeaway ending based on what this writer might have learned or how his life has changed.

Narrative Prompt: Tell the story about a time you did something wrong.

Wrong

If I could turn the clock back and change one thing about my life, it would definitely be what happened two summers ago when I went to stay with my grandmother.

My grandmother had always loved me so much. Her face just lit up whenever I would come for a visit. We did everything together. She taught me how to fish. She taught me how to shoot marbles. She gave me all of her old baseball cards. My grandmother was cool!

We were messing around in the attic one day and she found my uncle's old slingshot. "Can I have it?" I asked.

"If you promise not to shoot at living things," she told me.

I should have listened to her warning. At first I shot the sling shot at old bottles and tin cans that I lined up on the fence. I shot at milk bottles I filled with water and lined up across the driveway. Later, when my grandmother wasn't around, I would shoot at the squash and zucchini she had growing in the garden.

But one day while I was shooting, Grandmother's white cat, Susie, was walking across the back yard, chasing a butterfly that would light on the bushes. I thought I could hit the butterfly with my slingshot. I put a marble in the sling and drew way back on the rubber band. The butterfly flew off, and just as it did, Susie stepped forward.

The marble hit Susie in the eye. You can't imagine how I dreaded telling my grandmother. That cat was her whole world when I wasn't there.

The vet tried to save Susie's eye but he couldn't. He had to operate to remove her eye. I told my grandmother I was sorry, but that night I heard her crying in her room, crying like she could never stop.

_____

_____

_____

_____

Takeaway Ending Practice #3

Read the following **expository** piece. Write a takeaway ending based on what this writer has learned about elephant care and retirement.

Expository Prompt: Write about an interesting place.

Elephant Heaven

Imagine a place where old, overworked elephants can go to have a rest. The Elephant Sanctuary in Tennessee is just such a place. As a matter of fact, it's an elephant paradise!

All around the world elephants work in circuses. For a while they come out and amuse people with their tricks and dancing. They look happy in the bright lights with pretty ladies on their backs. But backstage they are sometimes mistreated and underfed. They work each day to lift the heavy poles that raise the huge circus tents. The rest of the time they are chained to a stake or kept in a small enclosure. Some bear scars and broken bones from harsh treatment. This goes on for 30-40 long years until the elephants are old or dying.

A group of people in Hohenwald, Tennessee, now have an elephant sanctuary where female elephants can go when they retire from circuses and animal exhibits. Their specialty is helping old, sick, or needy elephants. The elephant sanctuary is thousands of acres big so the elephants can roam and eat and become friends with the other elephants. There are woods, lakes, sand pits, and open fields. Talk about a neat place!

The elephants are bathed, doctored, and given huge toys to play with. They are fed hundreds of pounds of grain, fruits and vegetables, hay, and peanut butter. Special trainers work with each of the individual elephants to make sure they are given proper care and have their needs taken care of.

_____

_____

_____

_____

_____

Takeaway Ending Writing Sample

This kid, a fourth grade boy named Micah, has a great style for a narrative story. I loved his sizzling words and his clever descriptions. But there's a problem with the ending. Read it and see if you agree.

Narrative Prompt: Write about a time you had an accident.

Hey, do you want to hear the most contagiously, ...spectacular event EVER? Well, you have reached the perfect spot. Let me paint a picture for you.

It all started when I, Micah, was...well..about four years old, to be exact. Man, I was a prrretty young daredevil. I would eat bugs, squish a bumblebee with my bare hands, sleep under my bed. I would do just about anything if someone dared me to, and I mean you might think I was just plain BAD TO THE BONE, but in this story.....I WAS WORSE!!!

One sunny afternoon where the birds are chirping, the rabbits are prancing peaceful in the dazzling green grass...one little boy named Micah, still hasn't shown ANY fear, not even an iensy wiensy twitch!!

One of my neighbors across the street exclaimed, "Ha ha, hey Micah! I dare you to go to the tallest, MOST GIGANTIC staircase in your house and bounce like a pogo stick off the top of your stairs." I zipped through wind bragging in a competitive voice, "Bring it on!"

So, I bulldozed off of the stairs and KABLAMERS, I cracked my chin. Blood was leaking everywhere. I just said, "ouch" and fainted.

On the other hand, I woke up and I was in the hospital with thirty-two stitches in my chin.

Man, I remember that day like it was thirty seconds ago.

So, pull up a whoopie and I'll tell you the rest. Rrrrp I mean chair...Oh No look down there could it be. THE END!!!

The last few sentences are a huge let-down. It sounds pretty dumb when compared to the beginning and middle of the piece. It sounds like the writer got to the end and didn't know how to end his paper. Worse, it might cause a lower score.

I challenged Micah to write a better ending. He did! It's short, but it works:

Well, I learned to never try to leap stairs again or I will have the nickname, "Megachin!"

Florida Writes Format and Organization

Question: Do I have to write five paragraphs to get a good score on Florida Writes?

Answer: No. The people who score your paper will not be looking for 5 paragraphs. They will be looking for a beginning, middle, and an ending. If you've written a 5-paragraph essay and it has a beginning, middle, and an ending, that's fine.

Question: Could my story be one long paragraph?

Answer: Technically, yes. While it would be nice to have multiple paragraphs, the scorers are mainly looking for a clear beginning, a middle filled with details, and an ending that wraps things up.

Question: Could my piece be three or four paragraphs? Or six or seven?

Answer: Of course you can, as long as there's a beginning, middle, and an ending.

Question: Is indenting important? Will I get a low score if I forget to indent?

Answer: Indenting is always important. Be sure to indent at least the first paragraph, so you can show off the fact that you know how to indent. It would be great if you remember to indent the other paragraphs, but remember: this is a rough draft. The scorers are not necessarily looking for perfect indentation.

Question: Should I just start writing as soon as I read the prompt?

Answer: No! It's much better to think and pre-plan for a while. No general would go into battle without planning. No mountain climber would start for the top without first examining the face of the mountain and planning his strategy. No builder would start laying brick or pouring wet cement without first carefully examining and studying the architect's plans.

Question: If I make a mistake, will they give me another sheet to start over with?

Answer: No. Don't worry about mistakes! If you make a boo-boo, just cross it out and keep going. If you need to, you can draw arrows, write in the margins, cross out a word, and write a better word above it, or add more at the beginning or end. As long as your reader can follow your "road signs," you'll be okay. Great writing is more important than perfection.

Question: Do I have to write in cursive writing?

Answer: You may print or write in cursive writing. Your handwriting needs to be neat enough so that the people scoring your paper can read it easily.

Question: Do I have to have a title?

Answer: No, you do not have to have a title. Concentrate on the prompt, not on a title. Only final drafts have to have titles and Florida Writes is a rough draft.

Terrific Table Tents to Make!

You can make a really cool table tent to use on your desk. It's a handy tool to have when you write. One tent is for **expository** writing, and one is for **narrative** writing.

Instructions for Making Table Tents

For this project you'll need:

scissors   stiff paper
tape   1 copy of the table tents on the next page, p. 59.

1. Copy the table tent pattern on the next page onto heavy paper. Make sure to run off the pictures so they appear in color. Or, you can color the pictures with markers.

2. Cut down the middle of the page, so you have two strips. One should say Writing to EXPLAIN at the bottom. The other should say Writing to TELL A STORY at the bottom.

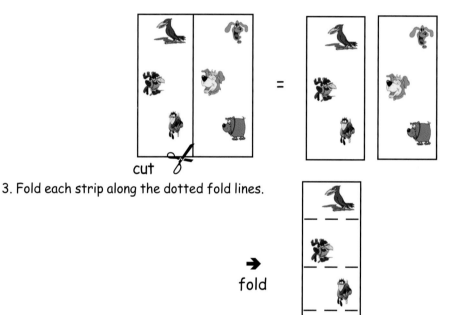

cut

3. Fold each strip along the dotted fold lines.

→ fold

4. Form the folded strip into a tent.

↘ fold over

side

5. Tape the bottom strip up over the top.

front   middle   ending

6. Flip the tent on your desk as you plan your beginning, middle, and ending!

BEGINNING

Tell what your expository essay is about.

- - - - - - - - - - - - - -

MIDDLE
(Choose 4 or 5 ideas, or add your own)

Describe your subject.
Write why you like it or
don't like it.
Write how it works.
Write something you know about it.
Write something interesting.
Write something surprising.
Write something exciting.
Write where it lives (or is).
Write something you have learned.
Describe how it makes you feel.

- - - - - - - - - - - - - -

ENDING

Write the most important thing
you can say about your subject.

- - - - - - - - - - - - - -

WRITING TO EXPLAIN

BEGINNING

Tell what your narrative story is about.

- - - - - - - - - - - - - -

MIDDLE
(Choose 4 or 5 ideas, or add your own)

Describe where you were.
Tell what happened first.
Tell what happened next.
Tell what happened after that.
Describe something you saw.
Tell how something made
you feel.
Tell something exciting.
Tell who was with you.
Tell why something happened.
Tell what happened last.

- - - - - - - - - - - - - -

ENDING

Write the most important thing
you can say about your story.

- - - - - - - - - - - - - -

WRITING TO TELL A STORY

Writing Terms Word Search

You deserve a fun break! Make your knowledge work for you. You've learned the 20 writing terms below. Now see if you can find them in this word search grid. Answers can go across, up, down, and diagonally. Give yourself 5 points for every answer you find!

```
P  J  L  M  X  Q  W  N  G  J  E  L  B  K  H  Q  V  C  T
F  K  M  M  Y  R  V  E  N  K  C  W  J  D  Y  T  V  L  A
N  T  K  K  V  R  M  N  I  K  N  M  R  M  H  H  L  U  C
X  T  T  W  J  D  Z  D  D  T  E  G  Z  I  T  K  Q  E  F
H  B  E  G  I  N  N  I  N  G  I  M  D  V  T  L  Y  S  D
P  Y  N  B  K  M  Y  N  E  J  D  D  I  N  M  E  R  D  C
R  N  N  T  K  J  R  G  Y  T  U  L  D  D  C  N  R  G  T
H  O  W  B  P  G  O  Z  A  G  A  L  T  L  D  V  Z  N  G
C  I  C  N  Z  D  T  L  W  C  R  G  M  L  D  L  P  I  T
O  T  V  N  N  E  I  N  A  T  Z  A  Z  Y  B  D  E  M  W
N  A  F  D  R  T  S  P  E  K  T  X  B  T  P  W  C  R  L
C  N  B  B  T  A  O  C  K  T  D  P  G  B  P  L  W  O  T
L  I  L  T  D  I  P  Z  A  T  P  T  R  W  E  M  M  T  K
U  G  F  W  K  L  X  X  T  F  T  F  T  O  W  R  L  S  T
S  A  Y  D  B  S  E  T  Q  G  R  L  V  M  M  D  M  N  Y
I  M  B  H  X  N  A  R  R  A  T  I  V  E  R  P  Q  I  J
O  I  H  C  R  E  A  T  I  V  I  T  Y  V  X  V  T  A  Q
N  W  H  F  L  O  R  I  D  A  W  R  I  T  E  S  D  R  K
R  E  A  D  E  R  T  K  N  B  P  A  R  T  N  E  R  B  R
```

Answer Key on p. 210

GOOD JOB, KID! DID YOU FIND THEM ALL?

audience
beginning
brainstorming
clues
conclusion
creativity
details
ending
expository
FCAT

Florida Writes
grabber
imagination
middle
narrative
partner
prompt
reader
takeaway ending
writer

Beginning, Middle, and Ending Paper

You'll love writing a rough draft on strips of colored paper and gluing them together so you can clearly see your beginning, middle, and ending.

Instructions for Making Beginning, Middle, and Ending Paper

For this project you'll need:

scissors	2 strips of colored paper
glue stick	1-3 sheets of colored paper

1. Cut two three-inch strips of colored paper the same width as writing paper. Use two different colors of paper, any colors that razzle-dazzle you. Choose a third piece of colored, 8½" x 11" paper.

2. Now write your rough draft.
   Write the BEGINNING on one thin strip.
   Write the MIDDLE on the long paper.
   Write the ENDING on one thin strip.

3. If you need more MIDDLE paper, choose another sheet in a different color. Remember that the middle is where you'll want to have lots of vivid details, examples, reasons, and mini-stories, so spend most of your time here!

4. Here's the neat part. After you've finished writing, glue the colored pieces together with a glue stick. That's all there is to it! Now you can clearly see your beginning, middle, and ending. This is a rough draft, so make as many changes as you need to. Don't be afraid to cross out boring words and substitute more sizzling words or to write in the margins if you want to add more details.

5. Hang these rough drafts from a clothesline or on a bulletin board for your fellow writers to see. This really gives you a "visual" of how writing is not just written off the top of your head, but is crafted and put together in sections.

Magnetic Panorama

A panorama means, "the big picture." On stiff paper, draw a big picture of some place you've visited, a field trip you've taken with your class, etc. Be sure to include things you'd like to explain and write about. This drawing helps you get your thoughts in order and actually see where you've been.

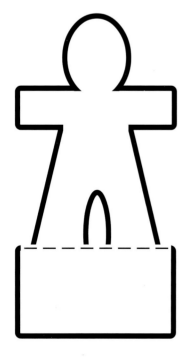

Instructions for Making a Magnetic Panorama*

For this project you'll need:

scissors	one paperclip	"paper person"
stiff paper	one small magnet	panorama drawing

1. Draw a large panorama on a piece of stiff paper. Include vivid details!

2. Copy the "paper person" on stiff paper. Cut out. Don't cut off the tab.

3. Fold the tab back under the "paper person" on the fold line.

4. Slip one paperclip on the tab.

5. Place the "paper person" on the drawing.

6. Use a magnet from underneath to move the "paper person" around as you talk about your drawing. You can draw a face and details on your person.

*This idea is from Mary Doerfler Dall's *Little Hands Create* (Williamson Books, 2004) and is used here with her permission.

Storyboarding

What's the best way to plan out your writing? In my opinion, it's the storyboard.

A storyboard is a series of boxes that can be used to divide your thoughts into different categories. When you draw little pictures in the boxes and add a word or two to each box, it's like a visual map of where you're going with your writing.

Have you ever seen a GPS system in one of the modern cars? It's the coolest thing you've ever seen! Right on the screen in front of you you see a map of where you're going. A recorded voice directs you so you don't get lost:

"Turn right at the light."
"Now, make a u-turn."
"Freeway entrance on the right."

A storyboard can do the same thing for a writer. It's perfect for planning a narrative story. It's terrific for planning expository writing.

Here's how to make your own storyboard:

Fold a sheet of paper into fourths, like a greeting card. Now, open it up completely. Fold back a little strip at the top of the long side. Fold back a little strip at the bottom of the long side.

Number the boxes from one to four. You now have four boxes to plan out your writing. As you get better at storyboarding, you can use a second sheet, so you have more boxes and more to write about.

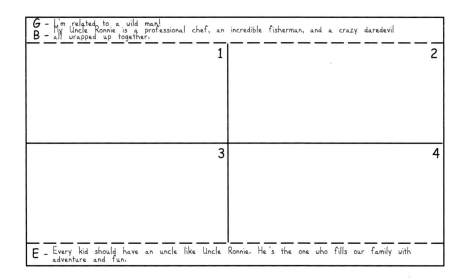

Start by writing a beginning sentence, **B**, across the top strip. Remember what we've learned about beginnings: short and to the point. Simply introduce your subject or topic. After you've written the beginning, write a grabber, **G**, above it. If you can't think of a grabber, skip it, and come back to it at the end. Sometimes, it's best to write a grabber last. Write an **E** across the bottom strip. This is for your ending.

In box #1, draw an icon, a very simple picture, of the first big thing you want to say about your topic. I'm talkin' S-I-M-P-L-E here. Are you listening? We're not looking for professional artists. Your drawing should take less than a minute to complete.

A word or two about your drawings: your drawings are for *you*. They're not detailed illustrations for your reader. The drawings are so you can focus on the topic and keep moving through everything you want to write about the topic.

You may write words or even a short list of words in the boxes. You can add dialogue. You can use jotting, if you like, so you can get your thoughts down quickly. This is fun!

Now, move on to the second, third, and fourth boxes. Draw simple pictures of other things you want to write about. You can draw several simple pictures or icons in a single box, each representing a different detail you want to write about. Just remember to keep "like-details" together.

When you have finished the boxes, it's time to write a wrap-up sentence on the bottom strip. Consider, "What is the most important thing I want my reader to know about this subject? Do I want to tell a lesson I learned? Do I want to look at important points and clues I wrote about and form a conclusion?"

Now, when you've drawn all the pictures and written on the top and bottom strips, then what? It's time to share your storyboard with other writers. In these months before Florida Writes, it's important for you to get lots of practice just talking through your story or expository piece. Practice telling your story, using your storyboard as a map or GPS system. The pictures you've drawn help keep you on track, keep you moving forward, and remind you of details you don't want to leave out.

Listening to the storyboards of other writers is just as important as sharing your own. "Beg, borrow, or steal" good ideas from each other. Professional writers do this.

Narrative Storyboard

G If you found a dollar on the ground, you'd pick it up, right?
B One time I played a trick on my friend Justin with a dollar.

1

Hey, let's play a trick on Justin

A dollar!

$1.00

2

$1.00

It's on a string

3

A dollar!

$1.00

E So if you find a dollar on the ground watch out: it might be me playing my tricks!

4

What?

$1.00

Ha Ha!

Expository Storyboard

2

4

G Do you know someone everyone wants to be like?
B My friend Doris is just that kind of person.

1

Pretty
smiles
thin
brown hair
glasses
stylish
comfortable shoes

Doris

kind
fun
funny
helpful
loyal
thoughtful
adventure

3

E I hope I am just as good to Doris as she is to me.

Blank Storyboard

1

2

3

4

Narrative Storyboard Questions

1 Subject: You had an accident
Box 1: What kind of accident did you have? Describe it.
Box 2: How did it happen?
Box 3: What happened next?
Box 4: What did you learn from this experience?

2 Subject: You learned to do something new
Box 1: Describe what you learned how to do.
Box 2: Who taught you how to do it, and how did they teach you?
Box 3: How do you do it?
Box 4: How does it make you feel when you learn something new?

3 Subject: You took a fun trip
Box 1: Where did you go? Describe it.
Box 2: What is something you saw or did there?
Box 3: What is something else you did there?
Box 4: What is your favorite memory from the trip?

4 Subject: Something scared you
Box 1: Where were you when you were scared? Describe it.
Box 2: What happened to scare you?
Box 3: What did you do?
Box 4: How did you feel after you were scared?

5 Subject: A super party
Box 1: What party did you go to? Describe it.
Box 2: Who else was at the party?
Box 3: What is something that happened at the party?
Box 4: Why did you like the party?

6 Subject: Oops! How embarrassing!
Box 1: Where were you when the embarrassing thing happened?
Box 2: What happened? Describe it.
Box 3: Who saw you or was with you?
Box 4: How did you feel when this happened?

7 Subject: You had a great day at school
Box 1: When was your great day at school, and who was with you?
Box 2: What happened on your great day? Describe it.
Box 3: What is something else that happened?
Box 4: Why will you always remember your great day?

...Narrative Storyboard Questions

8 Subject: You helped someone

Box 1: Who did you help? Describe him.

Box 2: What need did he have?

Box 3: What were the things you did to help him?

Box 4: How did you feel when the job was done?

9 Subject: You visited someone

Box 1: Describe the person you visited.

Box 2: What is your relationship to this person?

Box 3: What are several things you did together?

Box 4: What was the highlight of your visit?

10 Subject: You ruined something that didn't belong to you

Box 1: Describe the object you ruined.

Box 2: Tell how you happened to have it.

Box 3: Tell what happened that caused it to be ruined.

Box 4: What did you learn from this experience?

11 Subject: You had a magic carpet ride (imaginary)

Box 1: Describe the carpet and how you found it.

Box 2: Tell where you went on the carpet and what the ride felt like.

Box 3: Tell several highlights of your imaginary trip.

Box 4: Describe your return home, and what has become of the carpet.

12 Subject: You swam with dolphins (imaginary)

Box 1: How were you chosen to have this experience?

Box 2: Describe your favorite dolphin, so we can easily picture him in our minds.

Box 3: Tell about several experiences while swimming with the dolphins.

Box 4: What was the highlight of your experiences?

13 Subject: You took a limousine ride (imaginary)

Box 1: A limousine came to your school, and you were called to the office.

Box 2: Tell who was in the limousine and how you had been chosen to meet them.

Box 3: Tell several experiences that happened during your limousine ride.

Box 4: Describe the very best part, or highlight, of your limousine ride.

14 Subject: You took a boat trip through a Florida swamp (imaginary)

Box 1: Describe the boat and how the trip began.

Box 2: Tell about some of the Florida animals you saw on the trip.

Box 3: Describe one exciting event that scared or thrilled you.

Box 4: Describe the highlight of this experience and how you felt about it.

Expository Storyboard Questions

Subject: One of your favorite possessions
Box 1: What is your favorite possession? Describe it.
Box 2: How did it become yours?
Box 3: Where do you keep it or use it?
Box 4: How does it make you feel?

Subject: How you get ready for school in the morning
Box 1: What are the first few things you do when you get up?
Box 2: What is the next main thing you do? Describe it.
Box 3: What is another main thing you do?
Box 4: How do these things help you prepare for a good day?

Subject: Someone who helps you
Box 1: Who is someone who helps you? Describe him or her.
Box 2: What is one way this person helps you?
Box 3: What is another way this person helps you?
Box 4: What does this person mean to you?

Subject: A perfect Friday night
Box 1: What is one thing you would do if you could? Describe it in detail.
Box 2: What is another thing you would do?
Box 3: What are some things you would eat? Describe them.
Box 4: Who would you share this perfect evening with?

Subject: A terrific job
Box 1: What do you want to be when you grow up? Describe this job.
Box 2: What is something you would do in this job?
Box 3: What is another thing you would do?
Box 4: Why would this be a great job for you?

Subject: An interesting animal
Box 1: Name an animal you find interesting? Describe it.
Box 2: How and where does this animal live?
Box 3: What does this animal eat?
Box 4: Why did you choose this awesome animal?

Subject: A really good book
Box 1: What is the name of the book, and who wrote it? Describe it.
Box 2: Who is your favorite character from the book, and what is he or she like?
Box 3: What is one adventure that happens in the book?
Box 4: Why do you recommend this book?

...Expository Storyboard Questions

 8
Subject: A country you'd like to visit
Box 1: Introduce us to a country you'd like to visit.
Box 2: Describe something about the country you'd like to see.
Box 3: Describe something about the country you'd like to experience.
Box 4: What would be the highlight of visiting this country?

 9
Subject: The worst chore
Box 1: What is the worst chore a kid could possibly have to do?
Box 2: Explain why this chore is so terrible.
Box 3: Explain each part of the chore.
Box 4: How would having to do this chore make you feel?

 10
Subject: A terrific place to eat
Box 1: Introduce us to your favorite restaurant.
Box 2: Describe the decorations and atmosphere in the restaurant.
Box 3: Describe the foods that would entice us to eat there.
Box 4: What is the main thing you want to say about this restaurant?

 11
Subject: A sport or activity you'd like to try
Box 1: Explain why this sport or activity appeals to you.
Box 2: Describe it for us, so we get a clear picture in our minds.
Box 3: How would you have to prepare to be good at this sport or activity?
Box 4: What would be the highlight of this experience for you?

 12
Subject: Your class
Box 1: Introduce your class as though you were writing a brochure.
Box 2: Describe the teacher and kids.
Box 3: Explain some things that your class does that are unique and special.
Box 4: Explain why other kids would enjoy joining your class.

 13
Subject: Your favorite television show for kids
Box 1: Introduce your favorite television show.
Box 2: Describe the main characters (one or two).
Box 3: Explain some highlights of the show.
Box 4: Convince us why this show is your favorite.

 14
Subject: A person who is your "hero"
Box 1: Introduce us to a person you consider to be your "hero."
Box 2: Explain why this person is so special.
Box 3: Describe one specific thing this person has done.
Box 4: Explain how you feel about this person.

Temporary Spelling

In a perfect world, everyone would spell everything right. But the good news is that we don't live in a perfect world. You don't have to be perfect, especially when you're writing a rough draft. And the writing you will do for Florida Writes is a rough draft. Some kids get all nervous and anxious about spelling. They can hardly get their thoughts down on paper because they're so worried about misspelling something.

Even adults don't spell everything correctly.
Adults make boo-boos all the time!

The main thing to remember is this: you are a neat kid with a wild, creative, vivid imagination. You have a story to tell. You have an opinion to share. You have some explaining to do. You have many things to say, and we want to hear them.

So, first and foremost, get your thoughts down on paper. Don't take the time to stop and worry about the spelling of a particular word when you're writing a rough draft. Jot down a letter or some of the letters of the word, or spell it like you think it might be spelled.

When you finish writing, go back and make spelling corrections as best as you can. Why?

We spell as many words correctly as we can for these reasons:

Good spelling shows maturity!
Good spelling is a courtesy to the reader!
Good spelling helps the reader understand!
Good spelling gives you power!

Here's an example of a kid getting his thoughts down on paper. Notice that for right now he's not worried about correct spelling. Some of his words aren't spelled correctly, but we can still understand his meaning.

My mom's lazanya is delishus. She makes it for my birthday and other special ocazuns. You should taste how cheezy it is!!!!

Now, the real way to spell lazanya is "lasagna." And delishus is actually "delicious." Ocazuns is "occasions" and cheezy is "cheesy."

But it's better to invent temporary spelling for a juicy, sizzling word like "delicious," instead of writing a word you know how to spell, like "good." Take a risk! Live dangerously!

Jotting

I don't know about you, but when I brainstorm before I write, sometimes I have too many thoughts at once. It's sort of like a brain explosion of ideas all going off at the same time. Wowie! I can't write fast enough to write down what I'm thinking. It's enough to make me crazy!

When this happens, jotting can be a lifesaver.

Jotting means writing down a few letters of a word.

hw = homework   byd = back yard   m = mom

Jotting can also mean drawing very simple pictures that stand for what you want to remember to write.

When it comes to prewriting, jotting can be your best friend. If you tried to write every idea, every sentence, and every word, you'd be at it forever. Jotting is much faster! It's sort of a "shorthand," and everyone has his own version. Anything goes!

Lots of adults use jotting to help them get their ideas on paper quickly. When they take down directions or write a phone message they aren't worried about writing complete words or even spelling things correctly. A quick picture or a few letters or words will do.

last summer rode plane
cool!!!
groomed horse
6 days
barn

Jotting helps you get your ideas down on paper, as fast as possible, without worrying about spelling or punctuation.

After you read a writing prompt, and before you start writing, you need to get your thoughts together and get organized. That's called prewriting. Jotting can be a valuable tool to help you in the prewriting phase of writing.

Sentence Variety

It has been said that variety is the spice of life. We all like a little variety in our lives. You might love giant ice cream cones, but you wouldn't want them 24-7-365.

Have you ever talked with someone who told a long story and kept saying something like, "And you know what?" or "And then guess what happened," every few seconds? Caramba! You feel like pulling your hair out or screaming from boredom.

Sentences need to have variety in the way they're written.

Raven-Symone is my favorite actress. She used to be on "The Cosby Show." She played Olivia, the granddaughter of Dr. Huxtable and his wife. She was the cutest thing you've ever seen! She was so smart and was like a comedian even though she was only four years old. She grew up and she has her own show, "That's So Raven." She is a good cook and very smart in real life. She's my hero.

We might enjoy reading about Raven-Symone, but it would drive us nuts if we had to read many more sentences that all started with "She." This writer needs to use variety.

When you're writing, change up your sentences. Start them different ways. Keep some short, and make others longer. Sentence variety helps keep your reader interested.

Notice how much better the writing is when we rewrite the same passage:

Raven-Symone is my favorite actress. You might remember her as Olivia, the granddaughter of Dr. Huxtable and his wife on "The Cosby Show." Cute, funny, and smart, Raven was like a comedian at only four years of age. Now that she's grown, in her real life she's a good cook, she's smart, and she stars in her own show, "That's So Raven."

There are many ways to construct sentences so they are each unique and interesting. As you write, remember to use a variety of sentence types to keep your reader's interest.

It is a good idea to make some of your sentences start and end differently.

Sentence Variety Types

1. **Subject First:**   **Clowns** work in the circus and make people laugh.

2. **Subject Last:**   Wouldn't it be terrific to be a **clown?**

3. **Description First:**   **Crazy, wild,** and **wacky,** clowns get paid for acting like maniacs.

4. **Adverbs First:**   **Every week, like clockwork,** clowns work at perfecting their gags and routines, so they keep improving.

5. **Compound Sentence:**   **David Solove was the boss clown for eleven years with the Ringling Brothers Circus, but now, he has an animal act at Busch Gardens in Tampa, Florida.**

6. **Short Sentence:**   **Those floppy clown shoes kill me!**

7. **Voice:**   **I think going to Clown College would knock my socks off! I mean, talk about a sweet job!**

8. **Gerund Phrase:**   **Crowding into a trick clown car,** as many as twelve clowns can appear as if by magic.

9. **Transitional Phrase:**   **You won't believe what happened next.** Two clowns, dressed like women, hit each other with gigantic shaving cream pies.

10. **Dialogue:**   When the ringmaster announced, **"Ladies and Gentlemen, and now for the world famous Ringling Brothers Circus Clowns,"** I knew this was the part I had been waiting for.

11. **Long Sentence:**   **The Ringling Circus used to have a clown college where people could learn how to put on clown makeup, how to fall without getting hurt, how to put together a costume, and how to do all sorts of crazy routines.**

Sentence Combining

This is such a cool idea. It's called sentence combining.

We combine things in our real lives all the time. We combine fresh vegetables, cheeses, croutons, and dressings to make a salad. We combine clothes to make a full load for the washing machine. We combine ingredients to make a pie.

When kids talk out loud, they never think about how long their sentences are. They just open their mouths and speak. And this works, most of the time. Sometimes they speak just one word. Other times, they speak in long flowing sentences.

When kids write, however, they often write in short, choppy sentences.

I got a new dog.
He's white and shaggy.
I got him at the SPCA.
We named him Homer.

When you read them out loud, you can hear how choppy they sound. A whole paper written like this would be torture to read. Let's combine all of the important information into one or two longer sentences:

I got a new white, shaggy dog at the SPCA, and we named him Homer.

Instead of these teeny weeny sentences:

I'm in the fifth grade this year.
My teacher is Mr. Palaski.
We're going to have fun this year.
Heather's in there with me.

Try combining the information into one interesting sentence:

Heather and I are going to have fun this year in Mr. Palaski's fifth grade class.

Sentence Combining Practice

Your turn. Read the following expository sentences. Combine all of the important information into one or two sentences. There are many ways to combine. Listen to the ways your fellow writers combine these sentences. You might learn some neat tricks!

Dale Earnhardt was a stock-car driver.
He was very famous.
He died in 2001.
He died on the last lap of the Daytona 500.

_____

_____

_____

I love to play horseshoes.
I'm pretty good at it.
We play on the weekends.
My friends and I play horseshoes together.

_____

_____

_____

An octopus has eight arms.
It has two highly developed eyes.
The eyes are large.
It eats mostly shellfish.

_____

_____

_____

I like chocolate chip cookies.
I make them myself.
I usually put in tons of chips.
They're delicious!

_____

_____

_____

A Feeling of Completeness

I once read a great book about two cowboys who went on a long cattle drive. They faced mean outlaws and dangerous cattle rustlers. One of the cowboys got shot with an arrow and needed to have his leg amputated. Every page was a continuation of their riveting adventure from Texas to Montana. As I read, I thought, "This is one of the best books I've ever read."

But, as I got to the end of the book, a strange thing happened. I turned the last page and...the story just stopped. There was no "ending" as we think of an ending. I was so shocked that there was no more to the story that I looked for missing pages that might have fallen out. But there were no missing pages, and I was left with a feeling of incompleteness. I've talked with friends who have read the same book, and they felt exactly like I did.

One of the qualities our readers are looking for is a *feeling of completeness.*

Completeness means having enough of a story, or enough of an explanation of the topic, to satisfy the reader.

When you're hungry, you long for a delicious meal that fills your stomach and satisfies your hunger. When you're thirsty, nothing but water or a refreshing drink will do. When a reader reads your writing, he's hoping to read something worth his time and to feel a feeling of completeness. The dictionary defines the word "complete" as: having every necessary part or everything that is wanted.

Zillions of kids write great beginnings. They start out the middle by describing super details. But after just a short while they sput-sput-sputter like a car running out of gas. The details become fewer and less descriptive. The ending is barely there. It's as though they were saying, "I'm losing interest. I want to quit now."

How can we keep our readers interested if we quit before we've finished with a BANG? Don't give up! Keep writing with passion and voice to the very end! You'd hate to go to an exciting movie and realize, too late, that all the best parts had been left out.

When readers finish your paper they should be thinking, "Wow! That was terrific," or, "What a neat story," or, "I just learned something by reading this paper."

Your writing doesn't have to be LONG. It does have to be COMPLETE.

Revision

"When you first start writing, just get your thoughts down. Once you've finished your beginning, middle, and ending, it's time to revise. Revision is not about spelling and punctuation, although those things are important. Revision is about the big changes."

Revision means improving your writing in BIG ways.

When you come to the end, don't just flop your head down and rest until time is up. Go back to the beginning and read your paper. Ask yourself the following questions:

 Do I need a grabber to capture my reader's attention?

 Is there an unanswered question I could answer?

 Is there a boring word I can change to a sizzling word?

 Did I support and explain the topic with plenty of reasons, details, and examples?

 Did I describe so that my reader can picture the examples and experiences I'm talking about?

 Do most of my sentences start with different kinds of beginnings?

 Does every sentence focus on the topic?

 Do I have at least four to five writing skills that add interest and entertainment for my reader?

 Does my paper have a feeling of completeness?

Revision Writing Sample

Here's a real writing sample written by a fourth grade boy. The writing is terrific. It's got a great beginning and lots of vivid details in the middle. There's even a nice takeaway ending. The only problem is, there's an unanswered question at the end of paragraph #2. Can you spot it?

Narrative Prompt: Write about a time you had an accident.

The Big, Horrible Accident!

Well, you may have heard of original, everyday accidents. But you've never heard of an accident like this. It all began about three years ago.

Mom had opened the slide door that led to our garden. Dad had gone outside with her. My brother, Ben, and I were on the couch, closest to the slide door. My other brother, David, was watching television. Ben and I foolishly shifted to the back of the beaten-up, gray couch, when Ben gave me a little push and...Wham!!! Seconds later I was crying my eyes out.

Mom had punished Ben while Dad got a washcloth. When he came back, he put the washcloth under where my skull was bleeding, and drove me to the hospital.

When my dad got to the hospital, he bought me a bag of chips. Then, when the doctor called me up, I had to get about five or six stitches. I felt the pain for a couple of weeks, but they all fell out after that.

I've learned an important lesson. Never go on the back of the couch. If you do, you'll be feeling the pain.

I loved the set-up for this story. I couldn't wait to find out what happened. The problem is, I don't know *what* happened. After Ben gives him a push...the author doesn't tell us how he cuts his skull. Does he go through the glass sliding door? Does he fall backwards and cut his head? The author needs to revise his paper so that this question is answered.

List of Creativity Skills

Imagine finding a secret cave when you and your friends are exploring. You shine your flashlights deep into the cave, scanning the walls, the stalagmites, the floor. There. Something shiny. A partially opened chest. Bulging with gold doubloons, strings of pearls, glittering diamonds, rubies, and emeralds. Hidden treasure! A king's ransom! The fortune of a lifetime.

The writing skills we add to our writing are like glittering jewels. They enrich our writing and bedazzle our readers. Each one adds its own beauty, its own radiance, to our writing. Who wants plain, boring writing when we can have gorgeous, irresistible sentences?

In the next few lessons we will learn a variety of writing skills. You can use them to add sparkle and splendor to the writing pieces you are working on.

As you learn and master each writing skill, check it off in the boxes to the left. As you use them in your writing pieces, put a check to the right.

Learned   Used in my Writing

☐ style

☐ similes

☐ metaphors

☐ emotion words

☐ sensory words

☐ dialogue

☐ transitional phrases

☐ comparisons

☐ avoiding tacky expressions

☐ supporting with reasons and details

☐ strong verbs

☐ onomatopoeia

☐ passion

☐ sizzling vocabulary

Style: Puttin' on the "Glitz"

Kids love to read. Me, too! I read lots of books that are written for kids.

Most of the time we want to read something that's got some "snap" or *style* to it. What is style? Style is putting racing flame decals on your bike so it looks cool. Style is wearing neat-looking shoes that everyone else wants. Style is using words and phrases that other kids copy.

When it comes to writing, style is that special something that makes you stand out from the others. It might be the way you start your piece...or the words you use...or the tone of your writing.

This writing is plain. It has little or no style:

I love making bead jewelry. Making bead jewelry is fun. You can make lots of things with beads. My Aunt Susan showed me how. I have lots of beads.

Gee Whiz! The sentences are short, boring, and too obvious. Where's the flair? Where's the glitz? Where's the style?

Now, the following piece has style. See if you can spot *why*:

Iridescent green...peacock blue...blazing scarlet...shimmery mother-of-pearl. Just about every single weekend you'll find me hard at work at my favorite activity on earth, making bracelets, earrings, and anklets. When my Aunt Susan taught me beadmaking she introduced me to an excellent hobby and a way to make money, too.

Notice the word choices--they sizzle! Notice the specific details--you can picture them! Look at the description--incredible!

Your writing is a reflection of you. Take the time to give your writing style. Choose words with the same care you'd choose candy from the store. Give your writing flair. Show off your style! Just as your clothes and hairstyle reflect your personal style, your writing can tell other people many things about you, even if you never meet them in person!

Similes

Let's talk about similes. What a funny word. Doesn't it look like the word "smiles" to you? Well, let me tell you, if you use good similes in your writing, your teacher will be all smiles! Using similes in our writing is cool! So what is a simile?

A simile is when we make a "point" by comparing two things.
We use the words "like" or "as" to join those two things.

Let's see some examples of similes. I've underlined them in these sentences below:

After sitting in the sun all day, <u>our car was as hot as an oven</u>.
The new boy in our class <u>runs as fast as a cheetah</u>.
My new <u>pillow feels like a soft marshmallow</u>.
Our <u>teacher drives like a NASCAR racer in his new sports car</u>.

See how easy similes are to write? Each simile makes a point: just how hot the car was, how fast the boy is, how soft the pillow feels, and how the teacher drives.

Similes are as easy as falling off a log!
When I write similes, I feel like a writing maniac!
My teacher is as happy as a pig in the sunshine when I write similes!

Sorry...I get carried away when it comes to similes. Not only are they delightful to write, but they add sparkle to your writing. Use your imagination to finish these similes:

My cat's fur is as _____

The bubbles we blew hovered overhead like _____

When we lost the game, I was as sad as _____

Dashir plays basketball like _____

The principal was as mad as _____

When he sings in the shower, my brother sounds like _____

This candy tastes just like _____

Try to add a simile or two to your writing every time you write.

A List of "As" Similes

As agile as a monkey
As alike as two peas in a pod
As big as a bus
As big as an elephant
As black as pitch
As brave as a lion
As bright as day
As busy as a beaver
As busy as a bee
As clean as a whistle
As clear as a bell
As clear as crystal
As clear as mud
As cold as ice
As cool as a cucumber
As cute as a button
As cunning as a fox
As dead as a doornail
As delicate as a flower
As different as night and day
As dry as a bone
As dry as dust
As dull as dishwater
As easy as A.B.C.
As easy as pie
As fit as a fiddle
As flat as a pancake
As free as a bird
As fresh as a daisy
As gentle as a lamb
As good as gold
As happy as a lark
As happy as a pig in a mud puddle
As hard as nails
As hoarse as a crow

As hungry as a bear
As hungry as a wolf
As innocent as a lamb
As large as life
As light as a feather
As light as air
As loud as a fire alarm
As mad as a hatter
As mad as a hornet
As neat as a pin
As nutty as a fruitcake
As old as the hills
As pale as death
As plain as day
As pleased as punch
As poor as a church mouse
As poor as dirt
As pretty as a picture
As proud as a peacock
As pure as snow
As pure as the driven snow
As quick as a wink
As quick as lightning
As right as rain
As scarce as hen's teeth
As sensitive as a flower
As sharp as a needle
As sharp as a razor
As shiny as silver
As sick as a dog
As silent as the dead
As silent as the grave
As silly as a goose
As slippery as an eel
As slow as molasses

As slow as a snail
As slow as a tortoise
As smooth as silk
As snug as a bug in a rug
As soft as a baby's bottom
As solid as a rock
As solid as the ground we stand on
As sound as a bell
As sour as vinegar
As steady as a rock
As sticky as jam
As stiff as a board
As still as death
As straight as an arrow
As strong as an ox
As stubborn as a mule
As sturdy as an oak
As sure as death and taxes
As sweet as honey
As tall as a giraffe
As tight as a drum
As thick as a brick
As thin as a rail
As thin as a toothpick
As timid as a rabbit
As tough as leather
As tough as nails
As tough as old boots
As tricky as a box of monkeys
As welcome as a skunk at a party
As white as a ghost
As white as a sheet
As white as snow
As wise as Solomon
As wise as an owl

A List of "Like" Similes

clings like a leech
cooks like a chef
cries like a baby
cuts like a knife
dances like a professional
draws like an artist
dresses like a model
drives like a maniac
drives like an old lady
eats like a horse
feels like velvet
flies like the wind
floats like a boat
irritates like sandpaper
itches like crazy

jumps like a frog
keeps a secret like a vault
laughs like a hyena
looks like a giant
love is like a red, red rose
plays guitar like a rock star
plays like an athlete
pokes along like a snail
roars like a lion
runs like a rocket
runs like the wind
screeches like an owl
searches like a bloodhound
sings like an angel
sings like a diva

slept like a baby
smells like money
smells like rain
smiles like a Cheshire cat
snores like a buzz saw
soars like an eagle
sounds like trouble
spells like a dictionary
stretches like a rubber band
swims like a fish
tastes like ambrosia
walks like a model
watches like a hawk
wiggles like a worm
works like a dog

Metaphors and Idioms

"Ladies and gentlemen! Boys and girls! Aging grandparents and tiny babies! Step right up! Allow me to introduce you to that daring duo of writing skills....Known to us here under the Big Top as.... 'Metaphor the Magnificent' and his impressive sidekick..... 'Idiom.' "

A metaphor is a comparison between two unlikely things in order to make a point.

Metaphors and idioms are very similar.

An idiom is a colorful expression used to make a point. Many metaphors are also idioms. Many idioms are also metaphors.

We use metaphors and idioms all the time when we speak. They're those funny expressions that add color and interest to our speech. They're colorful comparisons that point out just how beautiful someone is or just how much they are loved. They're those catch phrases that become a "shorthand" for another meaning, one that isn't said directly, but indirectly.

For instance, you might want to say that you've put more food on your plate than you could actually eat. To make that point, you say:

"I guess **my eyes were bigger than my stomach.**"

Or, when someone has spoiled a surprise, you might say:

"Laurie **let the cat out of the bag** about Danielle's surprise birthday party."

Metaphors can also form a direct link between two very different things to show that on some level they are alike. Can you spot the comparisons in each of the following metaphors and explain what they really mean?

My Seeing Eye dog Max is my very own super hero, for sure!
We pigged out on leftover pizza after school.
My sister, the little angel, didn't tell on me.
Mom blew her stack when she saw that we had spilled
      root beer on her sofa.
Can you believe what a snake Garth is? He tried to steal my idea!
Lance Armstrong is a machine! He eats other bikers for breakfast!

A List of Metaphors and Idioms

This list of metaphors and idioms will help you spice up your writing. Add to the list as you find other metaphors and idioms from conversations, books, magazines, television, etc.

A disaster waiting to happen
A light bulb went off in my head
A shining example
An accident waiting to happen
Beat around the bush
Blow your top
Blows me away
Boiling mad
Break the ice
Brownie points
Bubbly personality
Butterflies in your stomach
Clear sailing
Cool
Couch potato
Deep, dark secret
Diamond in the rough
Don't be a wet blanket
Don't end on a sour note
Don't fan the fire
Don't rock the boat
Duty calls
Dying to meet you
Elvis has left the building
Eyes are bigger than your stomach
Feelin' blue
Finger lickin' good
Flew off the handle
Food for thought
Get a life
Give the cold shoulder
Got up on the wrong side of the bed
Grab the bull by the horns
Grates on my nerves
Gung Ho
Have my head on a platter
He's a comedian
He's a headache
He's wearing some bling
Hit the ceiling
Houston, we have a problem
I'd give my right arm for one of those
I'm all ears
I'm bitter about it
I'm dead
I'm hooked
I'm in a jam

I'm in a pickle
In your face
Keep your eyes peeled
Keep your nose to the grindstone
Keep your shoulder to the wheel
Left a bad taste in my mouth
Left high and dry
Let me chew on it for a while
Let me unchain my dog
My memory is a bit cloudy
My neck of the woods
Off on a wild goose chase
Off the chain
Off the hook
On the right track
Out of the woods
Pass the buck
Piece of work
Raining cats and dogs
Road hog
Rug rat
Running on empty
She can dish it out but she can't take it
She's 24 karat gold
She's sweet
She's the bomb
She's the cat's pajamas
She's the picture of health
Showered me with gifts
Something smells fishy
Spitting image
Steer clear
Step up to the plate
Swallow your pride
Talk a mile a minute
Tell me something juicy
That stinks
The light of my life
The real deal
The whole enchilada
Things are in a whirlwind around here
This homework is a breeze
Three dog night
Velvet voice
What a joke
Worked his magic
You could knock me over with a feather

Specific Emotion Words and Their Causes

"Emotions. We all have emotions. We feel emotions every day. Our emotions change with our moods and our circumstances. We relate to other people through our emotions. For instance, if we hear that someone's house has burned down, we feel sorry for the people who lived there. We feel happy for a family who wins a two-week cruise. Okay, so we might be a little jealous of that."

When we write, we need to tell our reader what we feel and why we feel that way. The problem, though, is that sometimes we are not specific enough when we express our emotions in writing.

We say:

I *felt good*........when what we mean is........I *felt proud of myself*

I *felt bad*..........when what we mean is........I *felt depressed about it*

I *felt awful*......when what we mean is.......I *felt ashamed of myself*

I *felt great*.......when what we mean is......I *felt excited and happy*

The more specific we are when we express our emotions, the more mature our writing. When we explain **what we feel**, we are being good communicators. When we express **why we feel that way,** it helps us connect with our readers. Here's what it looks like to express specific emotion words and their causes in our writing:

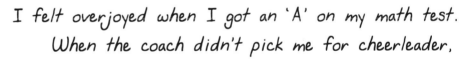

I *felt overjoyed when I got an 'A' on my math test.*
When the coach didn't pick me for cheerleader,
I felt rejected and left out.
Can you imagine how embarrassed I felt when
I missed the bus?
I *got a new iPod for my birthday. What a surprise!*

Emotions can be positive:

happy, surprised, overjoyed, radiant, loved, blissful, fulfilled, included, noticed, recognized, appreciated, relieved, adored, respected, peaceful, satisfied, delighted

Emotions can be negative:

sad, ugly, ashamed, embarrassed, humiliated, disrespected, nervous, worried, crushed, heartbroken, fearful, angry, dishonest, hurt, rejected, upset, disappointed, selfish

Emotion Word Practice

Dig into your sizzling vocabulary! Tap into your creativity!
It's time to practice those specific emotion words and their causes.

Write an **emotion word** for these causes:

When my hamster died I felt _____.

At my sister's wedding, I felt _____ when I saw her coming

     down the aisle in her beautiful white dress and her lacy veil.

When Grandpa asks me to go crabbing with him I feel so _____.

Don't ask me to do two things at once! It makes me feel _____.

I have a dentist appointment next week and I feel _____ about it.

I feel _____ because we're going to Animal Kingdom on Saturday.

I _____ going to my Uncle Sal's farm. What a blast!

No one knows how _____ I feel when I have to give a speech.

Write a **cause** for these emotions:

     I feel excited when _____.

      When _____, I feel relieved.

It's disappointing because _____.

Last week I felt overjoyed when _____.

It's kind of humiliating when _____.

My mother makes me feel special when _____.

I disappointed myself when I _____.

Boy, am I ever furious when _____.

Specific Sensory Words

When we write we tend to use only two of our senses: our sight and our hearing. We describe what we see and what we hear. Don't let your reader miss out on the three other main senses: taste, smell, and touch.

Let's say your class has visited a swamp. That would be an adventuresome, fascinating field trip! Your reader might never have been to a swamp. Tell him **what it looks like**:

dark
creepy
muddy
filled with cypress knees

green, thick water
snakes
gators
birds

And what it sounds like:

birds calling
raccoons chirping
squirrels scolding

gators bellowing
water lapping
palmetto fronds rustling

What excellent descriptions! But what about our sense of smell? A swamp has distinct odors associated with it that would make it seem more real for your reader:

the musky smell of rotted wood
the earthy smell of muddy water

the woodsy smell of trees
the sweet stench of rotted fruit

Don't forget the sense of touch. There are many different textures in the swamp:

squishy mud between your toes
the prickly surface of a pine tree
salty sweat on your face and arms

an irritating swarm of gnats
the trickle of sweat on your face
twigs breaking beneath your feet

We'd really have to concentrate to bring in the sense of taste where a swamp is concerned, but we might be able to do it:

the icy swig of bottled water
the tangy sweetness of juice
    from a juice box

the taste of salt in the air
the weird taste of a bug
    that flew in my mouth!

We have five senses. Use them creatively and watch your score go up, up, UP!

Sensory Word Practice

Read the following locations. Try to list as many descriptive sensory words as you can think of. Use your imagination! Use your senses! Create word pictures for your reader.

A shopping mall

SEE: _____
_____
_____
_____

HEAR: _____
_____
_____
_____

SMELL _____
_____
_____
_____

TOUCH: _____
_____
_____

TASTE: _____
_____
_____
_____

Take turns reading your sensory descriptions. Put the best ones on the board. Help each other improve. Give and share ideas and word choices. Create a "sensory award" for the writer who paints the best "mind-movie" in each of the five categories.

One to Two Lines of Dialogue

Dialogue. Man, that is one big $20 word! It may be tricky to spell, but it's simple to explain. Dialogue means talking. Talking is always interesting. When we write, it's a good idea to include one or two lines of dialogue for our readers because it adds interest. Here are some examples of dialogue:

1. Our bus driver bellowed, "I told you kids to sit down while the bus is moving!"

2. Meredyth asked, "Pardon me. Would you please pass the Grey Poupon?"

3. "Baloney!" my father said when I tried to explain why I hadn't done my homework.

4. "Not too short," I told the barber who was buzzing my hair off.

Dialogue can be as short as one word or as long as a sentence. As you can see from the examples above, we add quotation marks before and after dialogue. The quotation marks let the reader know that someone is speaking. It would be confusing to mix talking with regular writing if you didn't use quotation marks.

When you are writing dialogue, you also need some punctuation marks. If a person says a word, a phrase, or a regular sentence, and there's a speaker tag, you'll need a comma inside the quotation marks:

"I'll clear the table when this show is over," I said.
"Okay," Mom said.

If a person says a word, a phrase, or a regular sentence, and there is no speaker tag, you'll need a period inside the quotation marks:

"I'll clear the table when this show is over."
"Okay."

"That football player is like...so cute!"

If a person is asking a question, you'll need a question mark:

"Where?" Jacob asked. "Are we meeting at Wal-Mart?"

If a person is shouting or excited, you'll need an exclamation point:

"We won!" I screamed. "We won! We won! We WON!!!"
"We beat the Bulldogs 26-0!" Diego yelled.

...Dialogue

Here's another curious fact about dialogue: you need to indent every time there is a new speaker. Notice how this writer has indented for every speaker.

indent ➤ "Let's go down to the creek," I told Benjy. "It's a perfect day for swimming." It was so hot you could fry an egg on my forehead. I don't know why, but summer in Florida is like an oven! Believe me. I live here.

indent ➤ "Yeah," Benjy said, "I'm ready when you are."

indent ➤ "I'll make some sandwiches," I said.

indent ➤ "I'll get the drinks," Benjy said.

Adding a line or two of dialogue adds maturity to your writing and makes it much more interesting to your reader. But beware! Sometimes kids write too much dialogue, and that can be boring. Dialogue can also "take over" a writing piece, leaving your reader confused.

So be smart--use a few lines of dialogue to make your writing exciting.

Use your imagination and what you've learned here to create dialogue for the following characters. Don't forget punctuation and quotation marks:

A nurse at the doctor's office: _____

_____

A race car driver: _____

_____

A lion tamer: _____

_____

A kid on the morning of a test: _____

_____

A judge on American Idol: _____

_____

Nemo's father (from the movie Finding Nemo): _____

_____

Take turns reading your dialogue. Put some on the board. Help each other improve.

Transitional Phrases

Let's pretend you are an adventurer like...say...Indiana Jones or Lara Croft. You are in an enormous cave which is filled with...breathtaking treasure. The find of a lifetime! You are perched on top of an ancient stone column, about to fill your pouches with strings of dazzling diamonds.

Rumble.

You feel the tremors first under your feet, then up through your entire body. Earthquake! You must leave the cave immediately or risk being buried alive.

RUMBLE!

You could jump 30 feet to the floor of the cave, but you might break a leg or die!

RUMBLE!

You need something to help you transition from the top of the column to the floor of the cave. I mean, like, RIGHT NOW!

You leap from the top of the column to a high stone bridge.

You grab a dangling rope and swing across the expanse of the cave to the top of a carved idol. You grasp a gigantic mooga-mooga leaf, hold it over your head like a parachute, and float down to the floor.

You need to get from one place to the next, smoothly. The high stone bridge, the dangling rope, the carved idol, and the mooga-mooga leaf become your *transitions*.

We have transitions in writing, too, and they're just as useful.

A transition is a phrase or sentence that
takes you smoothly from place to place.

You can have writing *without* transitional phrases. I read it all the time. But the most mature writers—writers who write with passion—often use transitional phrases to move their readers smoothly through their writing. Here's a short example, just the first few paragraphs of a narrative, for you to see how transitions "pull" you through the story.

<u>Let me begin</u> by stating something we all know: don't put off until tomorrow what you can do today. <u>Here's what I mean by that</u>. Never wait until the night before the science fair to start your science project!

<u>It all started</u> three months ago when our teacher, Mrs. Burk, gave us an assignment to do a science project. "Class," she said, "You have two months. That's eight weeks. Don't wait until the last minute!"

<u>Now fastforward two months</u> to the night before the science projects were due. I had forgotten all about the science project...

Transitional Phrase List

Here are some transitions taken from kids' writing. They're real transitions, but they sound natural, the way kids talk and write. You can use any of these or use other favorite transitions in your writing.

After a few days,
After all,
After that important step,
And another thing...
And that's not the worst thing!
And yet,
Another example is...
Another thing you might consider is...
Are you ready for what happened next?
As a result of...
At one time,
At the same time,
At this time,
But if you really want to know...
But it gets worse!
But there are other reasons.
But wait, there's more!
Can you believe...
Equally important is...
Even more important is...
First of all...
For example,
For instance,
From that day forward,
Here's another reason why...
Here's another thing to think about:
Here's another thing.
Here's what I mean by that.
Here's why...
Hold on, because it gets worse.
However,
I want to be sure to tell you...
I wasn't expecting what happened next.
I still remember...
I'd like to focus your attention on...
I'd like to move on to...
If you can possibly imagine,
Immediately afterwards,
In any event,
In fact,
In other words,
In the beginning,

In the first place,
In the meantime,
It wouldn't be fair if I didn't tell you...
Just think about it.
Later that day...
Let me begin.
Let me explain.
Let me give you an example.
Let's look at it another way.
Let's move on to...
Let's start at the beginning.
Let's take another look at...
Listen to this.
More important,
Moving right along...
My favorite...
My story wouldn't be complete unless...
Now fastforward to...
Now that I've told you about...
On the other hand,
Once I was in the attic...
Once when I was about six...
Other than that,
Perhaps...
Several years ago...
Take what happened to me, for instance.
That's why...
The best thing of all is...
The next step is easy!
The next thing I did took a lot of guts.
The truth is...
This is my favorite part.
This next step is a piece of cake.
To be honest,
To begin with,
To further support my idea,
To show you what I mean...
What she did next was the bravest thing.
When I got to the spot where...
Without a doubt,
You can't imagine what happened next.
You won't believe what happened next!

Comparisons

We've already learned similes. Similes are comparisons between two things, using the words "like," or "as," in order to make a point. Remember? You're probably using them all the time in your writing by now. Good for you.

I'm as hungry as a wolf that hasn't eaten for a week.
My mother's face is as smooth as a pearl.
I'm sweating like a horse that's raced 10 miles in the desert.
She's as jumpy as a cat in a room full of bulldogs.
Her voice boomed like thunder.

Similes are comparisons, but there are other kinds of comparisons, too. When we write, sometimes we want to describe something for our reader to picture. We *can* use adjectives, and that works, too:

Jeremiah had a huge, toothy grin.

This description is pretty easy to picture. But we can also compare the grin to something else that **adds to the description:**

Jeremiah's huge, toothy grin reminded me of an alligator's.

We could say:

A tiny bird landed on my finger.

Or, we could compare the bird to something else that shows how astonishingly small it really is:

A tiny bird, no bigger than a butterfly, landed on my finger.

We could use adjectives to say:

Old Rosco, the rodeo cowboy, had a face that looked tired and worn.

But a better way might be:

Old Rosco, the rodeo cowboy, had a face of wrinkled leather.

If your tennis shoes stink, let your reader know just how bad they stink:

My tennis shoes smell worse than a rotten skunk!

Avoiding Tacky Expressions

Don't get caught by the S.W.A.T. Team! They're looking for kids who rely on boring phrases, silly sentences, and tacky expressions. Keep these out of your writing!!!

SUCCESSFUL WRITERS AVOID TACKINESS! (S.W.A.T)

Hello, my name is...

Hi there!

...for three main reasons

My first reason is...

My second reason is...

My third reason is...

I'm going to write about...

I like to ride horses. Do you?

Oh my gosh!

I forgot to tell you...

Meanwhile, back to my story...

The End

Do you want me to tell you a story?

Okay, here goes...

Here goes nothing...

I hope you liked my story.

Well, time's up so I'm outta here...

And they all lived happily ever after...

And I woke up and it was all a dream.

And that's the end of my story.

I can't think of anything else to say.

Bye, I'm outta here...

See ya, wouldn't want to be ya...

Now let's hear your story.

So Long!

This is stupid but, oh well...

Supporting With Reasons and Details

All writing should include details. Details are used to paint word pictures and create "mind movies" for our readers. But details also have an important function:

Details must support and explain the prompt.

The prompt, of course, is the topic we are writing about. Let's suppose we receive the following prompt:

> Jobs and professions can be rewarding and enjoyable.
> Think of a job you might like to try when you are grown.
> Now explain how that job would be rewarding and enjoyable.

We know, this time, we got an expository prompt because it uses the words, "Now explain how..." So, when we write, it's our job to use vivid details that explain clearly. We must choose our words so our reader gets the best mental pictures of what we are writing about. We must be specific. We must provide examples and perhaps a mini-story or two that relate our supporting details back to the prompt. Remember, every detail must somehow relate to the prompt.

Here's an example of expository writing that **doesn't** do these things:

I'd love to be a firefighter when I grow up.
Firefighters are cool. They put out fires and do lots of things to help people. They have to go to school. My uncle is a firefighter. He works at the fire station in Delmonico Springs. Firefighters save people. They work hard. But they love it. I think people would treat me with respect if I am a firefighter.

That's enough for you to see that this would never get a high score! The details are too simple. They don't explain much for the reader, who would ask, "How are they cool? What makes them cool? How do they help people? Where do they go to school and what do they study?" and so on.

When you write to a prompt, be specific! Write clear details your reader can easily imagine. Specific details and reasons give your paper weight and explain the topic.

Choose your words carefully. The words, "cool" and "lots of things" and "help people" are too vague unless you explain them. And remember, explaining is our job as writers!

Reasons and Details Writing Sample #1

Let's look at that same **expository prompt,** the one that asked us to explain what profession we would choose. Becoming a firefighter is a super idea, so let's stick with that. But this time, let's see if we can put some "meat on the bones" of our explanation.

Expository Prompt: Write about a career you'd like to choose.

"9-1-1. How can I help you?"

"My house is on fire!"

These are the words I will probably hear one day in the course of my duties as a firefighter. Of all the jobs in the world, it's the one I think would be the most rewarding and enjoyable. Let me explain.

People look at firefighters in their fire suits, covered with soot, sweat, and grime, working the hoses and ladders, and have a lot of respect for them. While other people are standing around just looking at a big fire, the firefighters are the guys who actually climb the ladders, carry people out of burning buildings, and put out the fire. Cool!

Firefighters have to go to the fire academy and study for at least a year. They learn how to roll the giant hoses so they can unroll them in a flash when they're most needed. They learn how to fight different kinds of fires and how to move around safely in a burning building. My Uncle Mike told me that when he was at the fire academy studying how to be a firefighter he had to wear all of his equipment, which can weigh 50 pounds, and stay inside a smoke-filled building for 30 minutes. He couldn't even see! But, that's what firefighters have to go through in a real fire.

I think I would enjoy teaching kids about fire safety, which is another job firefighters have. Sometimes old ladies call the fire department to come rescue a kitten that has climbed a tall tree and can't get down. Can you believe firefighters have to do things like that, too? I'm an animal lover, so I would volunteer for that job if no one else wanted to do it.

So, 20 years from now when you see the fire truck pass by in a big parade, maybe I'll be there up on top, waving to the people in my town. I hope I am smart enough and brave enough to make it through the fire academy so I can fulfill my dream to become a firefighter.

Reasons and Details Writing Sample #2

Narrative prompts need the same support as expository prompts. Here's a **narrative** writing sample that uses specific reasons and details to support the prompt.

Narrative Prompt: Everyone has had a special day. Think of a special day you have had. Now write the story of your special day.

Whenever I think of a day that is special, really, REALLY special, I think of the day that I had a tea party with my neighbor, Mrs. Ferguson. Now, I'm not talking about an ordinary tea party. This was special. Mrs. Ferguson is from Aston-under-Lyne, England, and they really know how to throw a tea party there.

Before I get to the tea party, though, I have to back up. You need to know a few things about Mrs. Ferguson. She's old, and she lives two houses down from me. Her husband died, and she lives all alone because her only daughter, Joanna, died when she was ten.

Mrs. Ferguson was visiting our family about a month ago, and she surprised me by saying, "Anna, I would like to throw a tea party for you and your friends." I didn't know what to say. She said, "My daughter Joanna always loved tea parties." I thought it would be boring, but my mom gave me "the look" so I said, "Okay."

Mrs. Ferguson said, "You may invite six of your friends. Wear your best dresses, and be at my house at 3:50 on Saturday afternoon." I wasn't really looking forward to it, but my mom MADE me invite my two cousins and four friends. I worried they would think it was dumb.

On Saturday afternoon we all met at my house and walked down to Mrs. Ferguson's. I was a little nervous because I didn't know what a tea party was like, and I didn't know if we would have a good time or not.

Mrs. Ferguson's sun porch was decorated like a Victorian tea party. Soft music was playing in the background. The tables were set with beautiful china cups, saucers, and plates that looked like they had been owned by a queen. The frilly tablecloths went all the way down to the floor! She had white Chinese lanterns with white lights in them strung around the room. It was awesome!

The best part of the tea party was the food, of course. Mrs. Ferguson served tiny little sandwiches with smoked salmon, ham, cucumber, cheddar cheese, cream cheese, and egg salad. The sandwiches were on a tower plate that was four plates high! There was a tray of hot scones. In case you don't know (I didn't), scones are little biscuits that are served hot with butter, clotted cream, and jam. Each flavor of jam had its own jam pot. There was strawberry, apricot, and orange marmalade. On the bottom tower, there were all kinds of tiny little baby-size sweet pastries. They were so small you could eat a whole one in just one bite. I ate a million.

But a story about a tea party wouldn't be complete without the tea! Get it? Tea Party? Mrs. Ferguson served Oolong tea with little sugar cubes. We each had our own pot of tea and a tea cozy to go over the teapot to keep it hot. It was delicious.

My friends and I thought the tea party was the best thing ever, like a fairy tale. How could I have doubted? When we left I hugged Mrs. Ferguson and said, "Thank you for the best tea party in the whole world." Next time I'll say YES right away!!!!!

Strong Verbs

Everybody knows a verb is an action word or a "to be" word. But what you may *not* know is that there are weak verbs and strong verbs. The difference is what kind of "word picture" the verb makes.

A weak verb is very general. It doesn't paint a specific word picture.

My *horse went across the pasture to join the other horses.*

The verb is "went." "Went" is a verb, but it is a *weak* verb. It is not specific. "Went" does not paint a "word picture." All we know is that the horse travelled across the pasture.

A strong verb is specific. It paints a vivid picture or, "mind movie."

My *horse* <u>galloped</u> *across the pasture to join the other horses.*
My *horse* <u>trotted</u> *across the pasture to join the other horses.*
My *horse* <u>zig-zagged</u> *across the pasture to join the other horses.*
My *horse* <u>picked his way</u> *across the pasture to join the other horses.*
My *horse* <u>raced</u> *across the pasture to join the other horses.*

Now you can see that the underlined verbs are strong! In just a single word they show you how the horse moved from one side of the pasture to the other. We can see in our mind's eye what a horse would look like as it gallops, trots, zig-zags, picks his way, or races across the pasture.

So, instead of writing: The *baby was upset.*
Make your verb stronger: The *baby* <u>held his breath</u>
                                                  and <u>screamed</u>.

Instead of writing: My *brother* <u>hurt</u> *me.*
Try writing: My *brother* <u>ran over my toe</u> *with his bike.*

Weak verbs: I <u>ate</u> *my dinner, then I* <u>went</u> *outside.*
Strong verbs: I <u>wolfed</u> *down dinner, then I* <u>bolted</u> *outside.*

Weak verb: I <u>went to bed</u> *at midnight.*
Strong verb: I <u>collapsed into bed</u> *at midnight.*

Strong Verbs Writing Sample

Strong Verbs give a writing piece some snap, crackle, and pop. This boy uses some outstanding strong verbs that take his **narrative** writing to a higher level.

Narrative Prompt: Everyone has had an accident of some kind. Think of an accident you have had. Now write a story about your accident.

The water glistened under that hot summer sky. The beach had a nice, cool breeze. I went out onto the wet sand and started to look for sea glass.

After searching for about half an hour I decided to go boogie boarding. I took one glance at the surfers, got on my board, stood up, and started boogie boarding. When a surfboard all of a sudden came hurling towards my way, I tried getting out of the way but the tide shoved me back. The surfboard pushed me into the salt water. It filled my mouth and burned my eyes and my back had a sharp pain.

When I finally got out of the water the surfer gasped, "Sorry," and walked away.

I went on my boogie board again like nothing had happened. Ten seconds later a woman about five feet tall with a braid came up to me and croaked, "Your back is bleeding."

When I heard this I trudged through the water to my mother and spun around and asked, "Is my back bleeding?" I could feel myself shivering. My mother answered, "Yes." I was afraid she would say that.

She asked, "Why?" I told her about the surfboard. I went fishing for the rest of the day. From that day on I never went to the beach and got in the water when someone was surfing.

The trick is using some strong verbs without using too many. You want to sound terrific but not overdo it. When you finish writing, read over it to see if there are some weak verbs you can change to strong, sizzling verbs.

A List of Strong Verbs

angered
anticipated
argued
arranged
arrived
articulated
backpacked
backtracked
ballooned
bamboozled
bandaged
baptized
blasted
blotted
boiled
bolted
botched
bounced
bounded
bulldozed
bullied
burped
charged
chastised
chattered
chauffeured
cheapened
cherished
chuckled
clipped
conducted
consoled
constructed
corked
crawled
crooned
cultivated
decorated
delved
demolished
despised
devoured

diapered
disciplined
dog paddled
double-checked
doused
drained
dreaded
drooled
drooped
dusted
eased
ejected
electrocuted
enfolded
enveloped
erased
evaporated
fired
flattered
flipped
flirted
focused
french-braided
frolicked
frosted
fumed
glowed
goofed
grated
greased
grilled
groaned
growled
guaranteed
guffawed
gurgled
hammered
harvested
hauled
hiccupped
high-fived
howled

humiliated
iced
infuriated
irritated
jabbed
jackknifed
juggled
karate chopped
leaped
lumbered
luxuriated
magnified
manipulated
meandered
measured
melted
monopolized
mystified
oozed
outwitted
papered
parachuted
pasted
patted
pawed
peered
piggybacked
pitter-pattered
plucked
poached
pounded
praised
pranced
prowled
raged
rammed
ransacked
reassured
recorded
rejoiced
relished
rescued

ripped
rocked
rowed
rummaged
sabotaged
sanded
sassed
sauntered
scampered
scooted
scoured
scraped
scratched
scribbled
scrubbed
shaved
shivered
shrieked
shrugged
shuddered
side-stepped
slam-dunked
slapped
slimed
slithered
smirked
snagged
sneezed
snooped
snoozed
snorted
splattered
spliced
splurged
sprinted
squealed
squashed
squished
stamped
stampeded
steamed
stitched

strained
stretched
strode
stuffed
tangoed
tap-danced
teased
thawed
throttled
thundered
tickled
tip-toed
toasted
trespassed
trucked
tucked
twisted
twitched
viewed
vindicated
volunteered
wallowed
waltzed
weighed
whinnied
whomped
wiggled
wiped
wisecracked
withered
wormed
worshipped
wrangled
wrecked
wrenched
wriggled
wrinkled
yelped
zeroed in on
zig-zagged
zipped
zoomed

Strong Verbs Crossword

Sizzling Words for Genius Writers

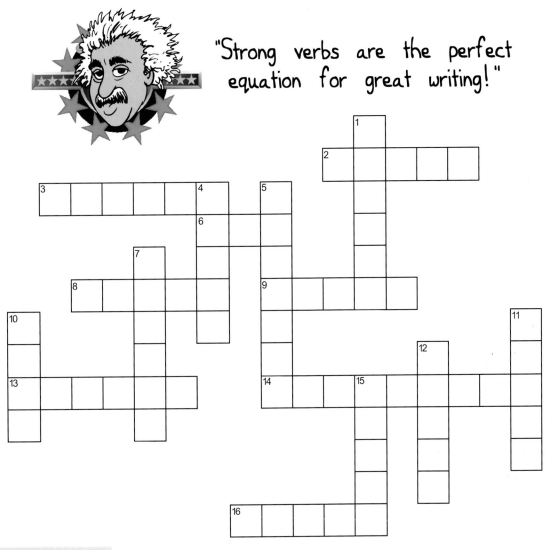

"Strong verbs are the perfect equation for great writing!"

Answer key on page 210

ACROSS

2 A stock car does this on the track.
3 A baby with an open mouth _____.
6 Hot kernels ___.
8 Wedding bells _____.
9 The sun or a cake _____.
13 Worms do this when they are on the hook.
14 A doctor has a room for this.
16 A clown's horn _____.

DOWN

1 Big diamond rings do this.
4 Fast skaters _____.
5 Stars _____ at night.
7 Great vocabulary words or strips of frying bacon do this.
10 Calves or babies do it when they're hungry.
11 Lawyers, coaches, and kids on the playground do this.
12 Some sleepers make this noise.
15 Butter _____ in a hot skillet.

Onomatopoeia

Sound effects. They rock!

My brother burped the biggest burp you've ever heard. Barrrrrrrrup! That kid can burp!

Sound words have a special name. It's hard to say and even worse to spell.

The word for "sound effects" is "onomatopoeia."

Yikes! What a word! But sound effects words can jazz up your writing. They help the reader picture just what it is that you want him to imagine.

Let's suppose you are a kid who has a great story to tell about the night lightning struck an oak tree in your yard. The oak tree then cracked in half and fell over, crashing into your room. You want your reader to know exactly what that experience was like and how terrified you were.

KABOOM! I woke with a start. A noise like a bomb going off made my heart almost jump out of my chest. CRACK!!! The sound split the air like an explosion. And then the worst of all: CRASH!!!!

"Dad!" I screamed. Something was filling my room in the darkness. Something was falling on top of me. Something big and leafy and wet. "Dad! Help me!!!"

This writing has passion. This writing has power. Sound effect words helped recreate the scene, so we could visualize it in our mind's eye.

As a writer, you want to use sound effects in your writing only when you need them to help your reader experience what you experienced. In other words, don't just use them any old time. But if you are writing about an episode where sound played an important part, sound effects words---onomatopoeia---can lend an air of realness to your writing:

I'd passed the bleachers many times on my way to school, but on this day, I heard a sound I'd never heard before. The tiniest mew-mew-mew. And then I saw it. A baby kitten, no bigger than my hand. His mew was no bigger than a squeak.

Voice and Passion

Every now and then you might hear someone talk about the need to have "voice" in your writing. That sounds curious, doesn't it? We have a voice when we speak. Do we have a voice when we write on paper?

The answer is yes.

Voice means "personality" on paper.

Each of us has an individual personality. Some people are outgoing. Some people are shy. Others say outrageous things. Some are funny. Some sound brainy and smart. When you hear some clever joke or saying that is being repeated around, you might think, "That sounds like something so-and-so would say."

Voice is an important part of our writing. Voice is what makes us sound like...*us*. Your writing sounds different from anyone else's writing. The words you choose, the way you express yourself, the feelings and emotions you write with, the subjects you choose to write about, all help to individualize your writing. They are unique, just like a fingerprint.

Without voice, our writing sounds boring and unemotional, like you're reading from an encyclopedia or a scientific journal. Whatever you write, write with passion!

How do you add voice to your writing? Good question. Here are some suggestions:

Write with passion.

Write from the heart.

Share your honest feelings.

Speak directly to your reader.

Use expression.

Try to connect with the reader.

Share a sense of who you are.

Remember that your reader is a real person.

Be conscious of the tone you are writing with.

As you listen to writing pieces your friends and classmates have written, listen for voice. Voice connects with the reader. Passion gives you the feeling that you are listening to a real person with feelings and emotions. Voice and passion can help readers overlook other "faults" because they feel connected to you and impressed by the depth of your emotions.

Voice Writing Sample #1

This **expository** piece, written by a 4th grade Florida boy, is oozing with voice and passion. Notice that some of his sentences are kind of wordy and might be a tiny bit confusing. Sometimes he hasn't spelled things exacly right or has a boo-boo or two in his punctuation, but his sense of passion carries the reader through.

Expository Prompt: Write about your favorite thing to do.

Some people like sports, some people like board games, but I like something much more intense. I like surfing!

Surfing is just like flying because of the thrashing white caps looking like clouds and the rapid waves swirling below your feet. It's impossible to hop off your board and go home. When your thrashing through the waves and gliding through the deep blue sea you feel like you have reached the unreachable an impossible goal. Last time I went surfing when I fell down like a bolt of lightning striking the sand, but when the waves were still soaring over me rapidly I thought that humongous wave was still worth it.

Surfing is more than a game for me, its life!! Surfing the best bond with man and water. It's more than putting a boogie board in the tub and standing up (And believe it or not I used to do that) its being the best you can be and being and doing the best you can do. When I was five and started surfing I wasn't good. My dad even had to push me so I could get enough speed, but I felt that God was lifting me up to heaven, and it was only the best I could do.

Not every one can surf so its radicle when someone admires you. if you do it, the way you can rip up on waves is sweet because it feels like your flying when soar up then stagger back down. It's hard surfing so when fall--bolt down like a rocket ship without something to slow it down. Once I fell down so hard and swallowed so much water I felt like they pumped ten gallons of water out of me.

People think that they will never surf like I did. Hey! but look at me!

Voice Writing Sample #2

Have you ever read a book and, by the time you finished, you felt like you knew the author? This personal **narrative** piece, written by a 4th grade Florida girl, has voice. She doesn't knock us over the head with it, like the boy who wrote the last piece, but because of the tone she uses, because of the things she tells you are important to her, we feel as if we almost know her.

Narrative Prompt: Write about a time you learned something new.

Horse Camp

Last summer I got picked to go to horse camp. I woke up and tore down the long steps. "Today is the first day of horse camp," my mom said.

"Yippee!" I exclaimed. I threw my clothes on and packed my lunch: water, carrots, a ham sandwich, and a cookie. I slipped on my midnight black cowgirl boots, then hopped in the car. Going to horse camp made me ecstatic.

When we got there a bunch of other girls were laughing, talking, and petting horses. The barn smelled strangely of hay. Horses neighed loudly. Then a lady came into the barn. "My name is Mrs. Holly. In horse camp you will learn to ride and groom horses," the lady said. We got to pick horses. I picked Pepper, a small white horse with tiny black dots.

We took the horses out and put their saddles on, then we picked out helmets. I climbed on Pepper's back and listened and waited for instructions. "To go, squeeze the horse's sides with your knees. To stop, gently pull the reins," said Mrs. Holly. I squeezed the horse's sides. I went too fast. It felt as if I was soaring in the air. I gently tugged the reins and we started slowing down. "Whoa, Pepper," I exclaimed and we stopped. Riding Pepper really got my heart pumping.

Then we got to groom the horses. We brushed them with a curry comb and a soft brush. Then we cleaned their hooves with a hoof pick and combed their manes and tails with a regular comb. We had a contest and Pepper and I won. There was no prize. It was for fun. I ate my lunch and then we had to leave. I'll always remember horse camp---the best day of my life.

Sizzling Vocabulary

When we speak, we use all kinds of really cool words to jazz up our stories and discussions. We want to impress our listeners. Imagine a group of skateboard friends talking about the latest board:

"You won't believe what Erica has."

"What?"

"The new Birdhouse Hawk Original Falcon."

"Radical! Did you see it? Did you touch this thing of exquisite beauty?"

"Yeah. It's one sweet board."

"Goo! What kind of wheels did she get?"

"Alien Workshops."

"Totally phenomenal! Do you think she'll let us try it?"

"I hope so. That would be most excellent."

Notice the buzz, the juice, the flow of impressive words. These kids are trying to impress each other. Their talk is rich and passionate. Yet when we write, we usually take the easy way out. That makes for dull, boring writing.

Erica has a new skateboard. It's so cool. I hope she lets me ride it.

Why do we do that?

Several reasons. We want to get through quicker. We don't think we can spell long words. We don't use our full vocabulary. Or, sometimes, we're just plain lazy.

Good writing uses mature vocabulary and interesting words.

It's the writers who refuse to settle for boring writing who get the great scores and impress their readers with sizzling words. Use snappy vocabulary words when you write. Of course, you want to be sure you know what these vocabulary words mean and how to use them so you don't look like a goober.

The kid who wrote the paragraph below mixes dazzling words, voice, and style into her writing with incredible results. Now *I* want to own a pair of Heelys! See if you agree:

Look down. Are there two wheels under your heels? Can you do a 360 in your own driveway in what looks like an ordinary pair of tennis shoes? Can you zip by shoppers in the grocery store aisle? Then you might be one of the lucky few who happens to own a pair of the most extraordinary shoes ever invented: Heelys!

Treasure Hunt Vocabulary Game

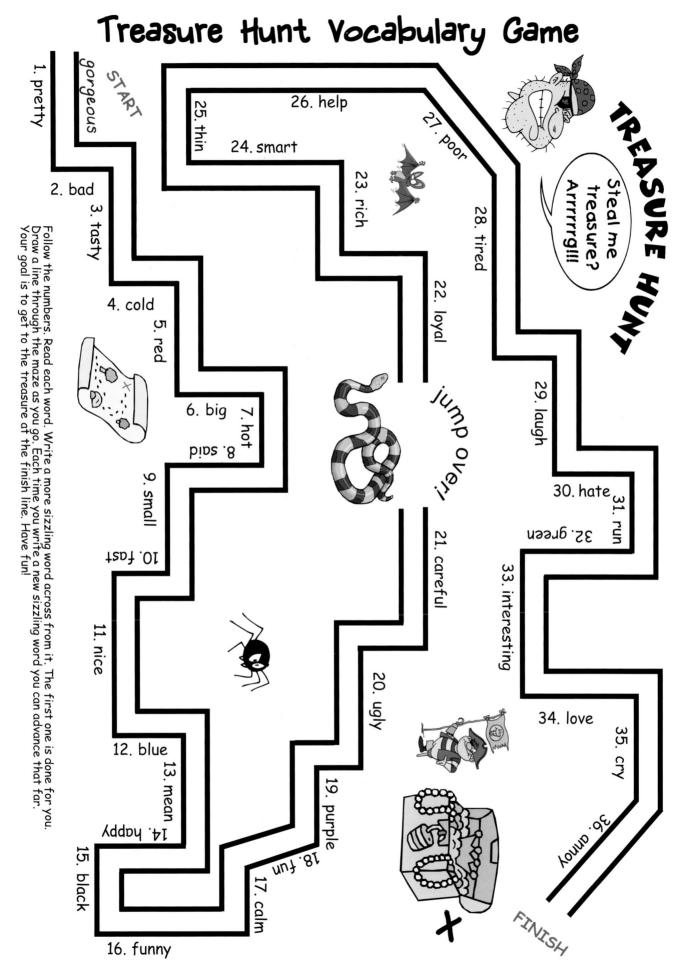

TREASURE HUNT

Steal me treasure? Arrrrrg!!!

START

Follow the numbers. Read each word. Write a more sizzling word across from it. The first one is done for you. Draw a line through the maze as you go. Each time you write a new sizzling word you can advance that far. Your goal is to get to the treasure at the finish line. Have fun!

gorgeous

1. pretty
2. bad
3. tasty
4. cold
5. red
6. big
7. hot
8. said
9. small
10. fast
11. nice
12. blue
13. mean
14. happy
15. black
16. funny
17. calm
18. fun
19. purple
20. ugly
21. careful

jump over!

22. loyal
23. rich
24. smart
25. thin
26. help
27. poor
28. tired
29. laugh
30. hate
31. run
32. green
33. interesting
34. love
35. cry
36. annoy

FINISH

X

Creativity Slider

Once you know creativity skills, it's a good idea to have a gadget or tool that helps you remember to include those skills in your writing. A creativity slider is just such a gizmo! With your teacher's help, you can make one in about half an hour. It's a handy tool to keep by your side when you are writing or revising a piece to make it score high!

Instructions for Making a Creativity Slider

For this project you'll need:

scissors	stiff colored paper, two colors
tape	copies of pieces #1, #2, and #3 from pages 111 and 112

1. Copy the three pieces of the creativity slider on stiff, colored paper. Pieces #1 and #2 can be the same color. Piece #3, the arrow, needs to be a different color.

2. Cut out all three pieces. Take your time so you cut right on the lines. Don't cut the arrow down the middle. The arrow needs to be one whole piece so you can fold it down the middle.

3. On piece #1, fold the side flaps to the back. Crease the fold.

4. Notice that there are two dots on either side of piece #1. Use your scissors to cut off the fold between the two dots on both sides. This means you will cut in just a bit and then cut a long thin sliver off the side. This leaves the side open. Do this on both sides.

5. Turn piece #1 over to the back. Tape piece #2 to the back of piece #1 so that it is closed.

6. Fold the arrow in half lengthwise. Tape it shut. You can use several pieces of tape to do this.

7. Turn piece #1 to the front. Insert the point of the arrow through the slit in the left side of piece #1 until it is sticking out the right side.

8. Pull the arrow all the way through the middle, until you get to the line of stars. A little bit of the arrow should still be sticking out of the left at this point.

9. Bend the arrow to the back.

10. Put a small piece of tape over the front and back arrow.

11. Bend the tip of the arrow to the front so that it points at the words.

12. Slide the arrow up and down for a handy reference of creativity skills.

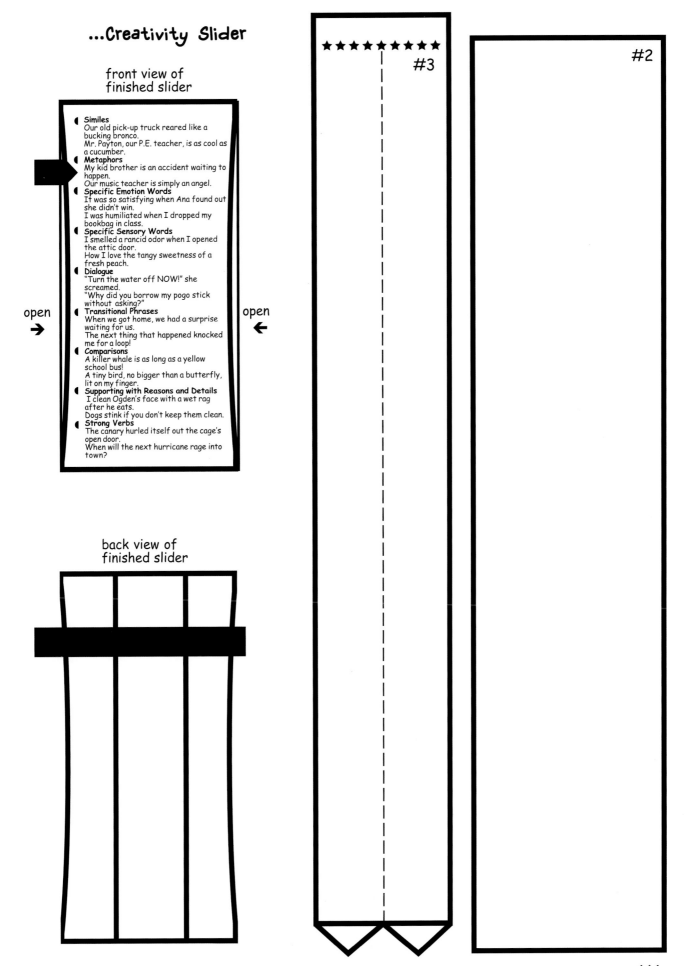

...Creativity Slider

front view of
finished slider

Similes
Our old pick-up truck reared like a bucking bronco.
Mr. Payton, our P.E. teacher, is as cool as a cucumber.

Metaphors
My kid brother is an accident waiting to happen.
Our music teacher is simply an angel.

Specific Emotion Words
It was so satisfying when Ana found out she didn't win.
I was humiliated when I dropped my bookbag in class.

Specific Sensory Words
I smelled a rancid odor when I opened the attic door.
How I love the tangy sweetness of a fresh peach.

Dialogue
"Turn the water off NOW!" she screamed.
"Why did you borrow my pogo stick without asking?"

Transitional Phrases
When we got home, we had a surprise waiting for us.
The next thing that happened knocked me for a loop!

Comparisons
A killer whale is as long as a yellow school bus!
A tiny bird, no bigger than a butterfly, lit on my finger.

Supporting with Reasons and Details
I clean Ogden's face with a wet rag after he eats.
Dogs stink if you don't keep them clean.

Strong Verbs
The canary hurled itself out the cage's open door.
When will the next hurricane rage into town?

open →

open ←

back view of
finished slider

★★★★★★★★★★
#3

#2

CREATIVITY SLIDER

Similes
Our old pickup truck reared like a bucking bronco.
Mr. Payton, our P.E. teacher, is as cool as a cucumber.

Metaphors
My kid brother is an accident waiting to happen.
Our music teacher is an absolute angel.

Specific Emotion Words
It was so satisfying when Ana found out she didn't win.
I was humiliated when I dropped my bookbag in class.

Specific Sensory Words
I smelled a rancid odor when I opened the attic door.
How I love the tangy sweetness of a fresh peach.

Dialogue
"Turn the water off NOW!" she screamed.
"Why did you borrow my pogo stick without asking?"

Transitional Phrases
When we got home, we had a surprise waiting for us.
The next thing that happened, knocked me for a loop!

Comparisons
A killer whale is as long as a yellow school bus!
A tiny bird, no bigger than a butterfly, lit on my finger.

Supporting with Reasons and Details
I clean Ogden's face with a wet rag after he eats.
Dogs stink if you don't keep them clean.

Strong Verbs
The canary hurled itself out the cage's open door.
When will the next hurricane rage into town?

Onomatopoeia
The bookbag ripped open and crashed to the floor.
"Wham!" I had been punched in the nose by a toddler!

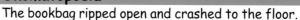

Sizzling Vocabulary
Miss Newell's engagement ring is absolutely exquisite.
I like to curl up in a plush, velvety blanket and read.

Descriptive Writing
Keyshawn braided my hair in long, tight braids.
The goldfish shimmered in the radiant sunlight.

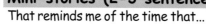

Mini-stories (2-3 sentences)
That reminds me of the time that...
For example, one time when I was playing soccer...

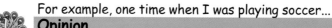

Opinion
Burgers are good, but in my opinion, pizza is best.
If you want to make me the happiest kid in the world...

Grabbers and Great Beginnings
Ben would never forget the day Martians landed in his
  yard and came in through his bedroom window.
Can you imagine owning a pet that can earn you money?

Takeaway Endings and Conclusions
I learned that when my little grandma says something,
  she really means it!
Balboa Elementary is the most awesome school of all!

fold

fold

Editing

As a writer, one of the most important things that you can do is revise your paper. As you know, revision means making the BIG changes--adding more, changing boring words to sizzling words, making sure you've used specific reasons and details to explain the prompt, and so forth.

But another important skill to learn and use is editing.

Editing means the little changes that make our writing tidy.

Just like you clean up after yourself when you make a snack in the kitchen or take a shower in the bathroom, you should edit your paper so it will be tidy for your reader. Editing includes things like spelling correctly all the words you can, starting each sentence with a capital letter, adding a period to the end of each sentence, checking your grammar, and looking for words you might have left out.

The most important thing you can do as a writer is to get your thoughts down on paper. After that, read it through. Make big changes that will improve your writing. And last, edit your paper. Editing makes you look good!

Here's a sample of writing that has not been edited:

Can you imjin what it woud be like to skidive I mean floating up in the ar woud be cool!!!! where I live theres this ar port and peeple skidive every saturday morning I want to take lessons! It coss $40 to jump with an instruktor and I have that much from my birthday but my mom said I haf to wate til im at least 14

The subject is exciting: parachuting. The writer writes with passion! Lots of kids would like to read about parachuting. But the lack of editing makes it difficult to read. Here's the same piece with a few changes:

Can you imagine what it woud be like to skydive? I mean, floating up in the air would be cool!!!! Where I live there's this airport, and people skydive every Saturday morning. I want to take lessons! It costs $40 to jump with an instructor. I have that much saved from my birthday, but my mom said I have to wait till I'm at least 14.

Editing Writing Sample

Here's a writing sample from a 4th grade girl. Notice how a writer edits her work after she's written, crossing things out, adding punctuation, etc. And get this: it's perfectly okay to leave those marks on a rough draft such as Florida Writes. Your reader will be impressed that you made the effort to improve your paper.

Narrative Prompt: Write about something exciting that has happened to you.

Oh NO! Not Another Hurricane!

The sky was growing dark, lighning booming out of nowhere. This storm's landfall was drawing closer. Hurricane after hurricane, those deadly storms started to appear right to where I live. Florida should be called, "Heaven for Hurricanes." I'm sitting here as Hurricanes Frances, Jean, and Ivan come to haunt me.

"Hurricane Frances has now made landfall near St. Marks, and is headed straight for Tallahassee!" I had the T.V. on channel 47. That's the weather channel for everyone in the USA. Hurricane Frances was finished doing her horror in Tampa and created a terrible present for Tallahassee. She left trees down at my neighbor's house and many branches and leaves on the ground. What used to be flying debris lay as still as a wall.

Later, Hurricane Jean came as I was in Tampa. I thought it would be a nice break from hurricanes. What I didn't know was that Jean was now making landfall close to where I was visiting. Jean finally came through and left us with practically nothing good. We were near the eye so there was flooding and a whole bunch of power outages. Because of that, the airport was closed, which meant I would miss my flight.

Whew! You'd think Tallahassee would be done with hurricanes by now! Hurricane Ivan brought us all the rest we needed! Ivan gave us many tornadoes, smashed sheds, and worst of all deadly news breaks. My family sat without power for what seemed like ages. The news cast got worried and more worried every time a hurricane made landfall. This had been the busiest hurricane season in years.

At last, all hurricanes this year came to an end. Hurricanes Frances, Ivan, and Jean had finally ended. They didn't just leave like nothing happened. It left a very sad but happy marks of relief and sighs that this was finally over.

Handwriting

Have you ever tried to read someone's paper and the handwriting was so bad you couldn't make out any of the words?

Or the writing is so small that you practically need a microscope to read it?

I have a green turtle named Rufus who lives in my room in an aquarium. I bought Rufus at the flea market in Daytona. He's a red-earred slider, which means he's a hard-shelled turtle with small red dots over his ears. Rufus eats raw hamburger meat and fresh vegetables. Once I even gave him an earthworm and he fell on it like a hungry kid eating a pepperoni pizza.

You may write the best piece ever, but if no one can read it, you're sunk!

If you can, take the time to form your letters so people can read your handwriting. Most kids can write pretty well with a pencil, but for some kids, writing with a pencil is torture. If you have trouble writing with a pencil, consider learning to use a laptop or an Alphasmart keyboard for your writing. We live in a computer world! You can find out about an Alphasmart at www.alphasmart.com, or talk to your teacher about the possibilities.

Now, I don't mean your paper has to look gorgeous and perfect. Not at all. It should be readable, though. When you're writing, you might make errors. Sometimes you write one word and then want to change it to a better, more sizzling word. Good for you! Just cross it out with one line. Don't take the time to erase when you're writing a rough draft.

If you think of something you want to add later and there's no room, draw an arrow out to the side margin. Your reader will follow your "road signs."

I have a green turtle named Rufus who lives in my room. I bought Rufus for $1.50 at the big flea market in Daytona. He's a red-earred slider, which means he's a hard-shelled turtle with small red dots over his ears.

Grammar and Punctuation

"If you want the HIGHEST SCORE on your writing, pay attention to these grammar rules. Learn them well, and you'll have something to cock-a-doodle-doo about!"

RULE #1

The words EVERYBODY, ANYBODY, ANYONE, EACH, NEITHER, NOBODY, SOMEONE, and A PERSON are singular. They take singular pronouns such as *his, her,* or *its.*

 This is incorrect:

Everybody ought to make <u>their</u> bed in the morning.

 This is correct:

Everybody ought to make <u>his</u> bed in the morning. (or her bed)

RULE #2

If you are writing in the first person (I, me, my, we, our, us), don't switch to the third person (he, she, they, it). You can refer to other people, but keep your "point of view" as though you are writing and seeing things with your own eyes.

Here is a writing sample that switches between first person and third person:

first person   first person   first person   first person
Yesterday morning my alarm went off early! I was glad, because my dad and I were
first personn   first person
going fishing. "Get your pole," Dad whispered quietly. I did. Then we were off, walking down
first person
to our favorite fishing hole.

third person   third person   third person
The sun was not up yet when they got there. She baited her hook with a fat worm.
third person
She cast it out and sat on a smooth rock to wait for the fish to bite. Suddenly, there
first person   first person
was a nibble. I yanked on my pole and quickly pulled in a fat trout. The first fish of the
third person
day! She wanted to jump up and down!

The writer begins by writing as though the story happened to her. Then she changes the "point of view" as though she is writing about someone else. This is confusing!

...Grammar and Punctuation

RULE #3

Don't use double negatives.

 This is incorrect:
We <u>don't</u> <u>never</u> have any fun homework anymore.

 This is correct:
We <u>don't</u> ever have any fun homework anymore.

 This is incorrect:
She <u>won't</u> lend me <u>no</u> money.

 This is correct:
She <u>won't</u> lend me any money.

RULE #4

When something belongs to someone, be sure to use apostrophe and then the letter s ('s) to show ownership.

 This is incorrect:
We're going by <u>Monique</u> house this afternoon.

 This is correct:
We're going by <u>Monique's</u> house this afternoon.

 This is incorrect:
That's <u>Eric</u> book bag.

 This is correct:
That's <u>Eric's</u> book bag.

 This is incorrect:
Maybe <u>Timon</u> brother will give me a popsicle.

 This is correct:
Maybe <u>Timon's</u> brother will give me a popsicle.

Your good grammar gives me something to crow about!

...Grammar and Punctuation

RULE #5

Use the words IS, AM, or ARE in the present tense (now).

This is incorrect:

She <u>be</u> my friend.

This is correct:

She <u>is</u> my friend.

This is incorrect:

We <u>be going</u> to the football game next Friday night.

This is correct:

We <u>are going</u> to the football game next Friday night.

RULE #6

Make sure your subject and verb "agree" with each other.
Agreeing means they go together correctly.

This is incorrect:

<u>She come</u> in late every morning.

This is correct:

<u>She comes</u> in late every morning.

This is incorrect:

Each of my brothers <u>paddle</u> the boat.

This is correct:

Each of my brothers <u>paddles</u> the boat.
(the subject is each, not brothers)

This is incorrect:

We <u>is</u> going fishing.

This is correct:

We <u>are</u> going fishing.

I MIGHT QUIT BEING A CARNIVORE AND START EATING GOOD GRAMMAR!

...Grammar and Punctuation

RULE #7

Every sentence must have a subject and a verb.

This is incorrect:

Over at the sunny, sandy beach in New Smyrna.

This is correct:

Over at the sunny, sandy beach in New Smyrna, I <u>surf</u> the waves.

This is incorrect:

<u>Plants</u> a new garden every spring.

This is correct:

My <u>Aunt Shirley</u> <u>plants</u> a new garden every spring.

This is incorrect:

Sometime in the future.

This is correct:

Sometime in the future, I <u>want</u> to go to college.

Don't call me a birdbrain... I use good grammar!

RULE #8

Separate a list of nouns, adjectives, or adverbs by commas.

This is incorrect:

The <u>hot</u> <u>crispy</u> cheesy taco melted in my mouth.

This is correct:

The <u>hot,</u> <u>crispy,</u> cheesy taco melted in my mouth. (adjectives)

This is incorrect:

<u>Tenderly</u> <u>lovingly</u> <u>quietly</u> I patted my baby brother to sleep.

This is correct:

<u>Tenderly,</u> <u>lovingly,</u> <u>quietly</u> I patted my baby brother to sleep. (adverbs)

This is incorrect:

I bought new <u>shoes a new shirt some socks and some peanuts.</u>

This is correct:

I bought <u>new shoes, a new shirt, some socks, and some peanuts.</u> (nouns)

Seven "Superstar" Punctuation Marks

 ## CAPITAL LETTERS

These guys are so important! ALWAYS begin a sentence with a capital letter. Use a capital letter for every proper noun or name.

 ## PERIODS

ALWAYS end every ordinary sentence with a period. A period is like a stop sign. It tells the reader he has arrived at the end of a complete thought.

 ## EXCLAMATION POINT

If you want to show excitement of any kind, ALWAYS use an exclamation point! If you're REALLY excited, use several exclamation points!!!

 ## QUESTION MARK

If you're asking a question, ALWAYS use a question mark. This is the sign for the reader to ask himself, "Hmm...what IS the answer to that question?"

 ## INDENTATION

ALWAYS indent the first paragraph of anything you're writing. For a final draft, you should also indent every time you introduce a new idea, a new speaker, change times, or location. Remember to indent before your takeaway ending or conclusion.

 ## COMMAS IN A SERIES

ALWAYS use commas between words in a series: nouns, adjectives, adverbs, etc.

 ## QUOTATION MARKS

ALWAYS use quotation marks when someone is speaking. You can also use quotation marks for special words or terms.

When to Use Capital Letters

Do you like to get attention when you deserve it? Do you like for people to clap and cheer when you do something great? Well, some words are just like that. They want attention! They want to be noticed! They want to start with a capital letter!

Be sure to use capital letters for:

CAPITAL LETTERS!!

AH!   WOW!

OOO!   oh!

The beginning of a sentence	*Someday, I want to take dancing lessons.*
Someone's name	*Thomas, Baz, Jennifer, Mom, Sarah, etc.*
Days of the week	*Sunday, Monday, Tuesday, etc.*
Months of the year	*January, February, March, etc.*
A brand name	*Hershey Bar, Cheerios, Capri Sun, etc.*
A television show	*Phil of the Future, Hannah Montana, etc.*
A movie	*Cars, Pirates of the Caribbean, etc.*
A book title	*Holes, Maniac Magee, The Reptile Room, etc.*
A poem title	*I Have a Dream, The Raven, Humpty Dumpty, etc.*
A magazine title	*National Geographic for Kids, Highlights, etc.*
A newspaper	*The Orlando Sentinal, USA Today, etc.*
A play	*The Lion King, Wicked, Phantom of the Opera, etc.*
The name of a city	*Palatka, Apopka, Two Egg, Palmetto, DeLand, etc.*
The name of a state	*Florida, Oregon, Texas, Alabama, etc.*
The name of a country	*Italy, Cambodia, Peru, Canada, Spain, etc.*
Titles	*Mrs. Wenton, Dr. Phil, Queen Elizabeth, etc.*
Colleges and Universities	*Florida State University, Stetson, Rollins, etc.*
Languages	*German, French, Farsi, Spanish, Creole, etc.*
Religions	*Baptist, Catholic, Buddhist, Methodist, etc.*
Ethnicity	*African-American, Hispanic, Asian, etc.*
Nationalities	*Irish, Dutch, German, Thai, Panamanian, etc.*

Sentence Fragments

If you drop a glass jar on the concrete floor, the jar will shatter into fragments, or incomplete pieces. A sentence fragment is just that—a piece of a sentence.

Complete sentences contain both a noun and a verb.

This is a complete sentence: *Shondrelle ran to the playground.*

This is a sentence fragment: *Shondrelle to the playground.*

Obviously the fragment doesn't make sense because it doesn't have a verb. This happens all the time in our writing. We get going fast when we write, and our brain forgets to put in the verb or the noun.

Now, when we speak, we often use sentence fragments, and that's okay. We answer each other with a word or two or a phrase. You talk to your friends, and you don't have to use complete sentences to make sense:

"Want to go snorkeling at the beach?"
"Go WHAT-ing?"
"Snorkeling. You know. Where you dive with a breathing tube and look
       for fish. You use a mask, too."
"Oh yeah. Cool!"

There are two times you can write with fragments:
       When you write dialogue
       When you write an aside

What is an aside?

An aside is when you "talk" directly to the reader in your writing piece.
An aside can be an expression.
An aside doesn't have to be a complete sentence. It can be a fragment.

The nurse came in with a huge shot. <u>Oh, brother!</u> *You should have seen it! I was petrified! "Time for your vaccination," she said in a gravelly voice. It was all I could do to keep from fainting. The needle was three inches long!* <u>Can you imagine?</u>

Sentence Fragment Practice

"Now's the time to show what a genius you are! Write C in the blank if it's a complete sentence. Write F if it's a fragment. Write A if it's an aside, which talks directly to the reader.
Give yourself 4 points for every answer you get right."

1. _____ The homework my teacher gives.

2. _____ Hulk Hogan is one big dude!

3. _____ The keys to my dad's car.

4. _____ "Dad, can I go with you?"

5. _____ Salvatore raced through the woods to avoid a swarm of angry bees.

6. _____ My best friend, Tamara.

7. _____ You're kidding!

8. _____ Ha ha!

9. _____ When I get home late in the afternoon after school.

10. _____ Wow!

11. _____ This summer we are going to visit my aunt in Botswana, Africa.

12. _____ Oh, brother.

13. _____ What would you do if you dropped your mom's diamond wedding ring down the drain?

14. _____ Yikes!

15. _____ Some of the time.

16. _____ My best friend John's dog.

17. _____ My favorite television show comes on every Thursday night.

18. _____ The new lady who works in the front office.

19. _____ "Not me."

20. _____ Since I'm the new kid at school.

21. _____ Get this.

22. _____ New clothes, a video game, some cologne, and a bracelet.

23. _____ A baby colt was born in the barn last night.

24. _____ "Yeah! Me, too."

25. _____ All the members of my family.

Run-On Sentences

Here's the truth: if you're driving and you run a STOP sign, you could cause a terrible accident and end up in jail. When you're writing, putting a period at the end of your sentence tells your reader to stop. Each sentence is a complete thought. When you forget the period, you have what is called a run-on sentence. This is a BIG no-no. A run-on sentence can be confusing for your reader, who won't know when one thought stops and another begins.

A run-on sentence is two sentences that follow each other without any end punctuation between them.

RUN-ON JAIL

Here are some examples of run-on sentences:

Tiki is coming over tomorrow night we are going to have fun.

There should be a period between "night" and "we." The word "we" should be capitalized.

Tiki is coming over tomorrow night. We are going to have fun.

If you've done this before, you're not alone. Even adults sometimes forget to put in punctuation and capital letters and end up with run-on sentences. The problem is, run-ons confuse your readers and make you look like you don't know how to write a proper sentence.

Read the following writing sample. Add periods and capital letters between any run-on sentences. Can you find them? There are three.

Have you seen "The Suite Life of Zach and Cody?" It's my favorite show and boy, is it good it's about two twin brothers who live in a swanky hotel. Their mother is a singer at the hotel and their family gets to live in an elegant suite. The girl who runs the gift shop also babysits for the boys she gets them out of trouble when they get into trouble. They do get into trouble and have adventures, all over the hotel the daughter of the hotel owner is London, and she is very rich and spoiled. Zach and Cody aren't spoiled they just like to have fun.

Punctuation Practice #1

"Don't be crabby! Now YOU get to be the teacher. Find and correct the errors below. When your teacher gives you the right answers, check the box and give yourself 5 points for every one you get right. If you get them ALL right, give yourself an extra 100 points! You rock, Dude!"

1. "Do you want to exchange marbles with me" Jacob asked.

2. Yes, Jacob said.

3. Later on this afternoon.

4. My sister isn't getting no presents for her birthday.

5. I'm getting my hair cut tomorrow I found a real cute style I want.

6. Does everyone have their lunch?

7. I bought this bunch of balloons for kenisha.

8. Would you like to come with us to the beach?

9. The kitchen is on fire

10. I used my money at the flea market to buy kettle corn baseball cards and sunglasses.

11. Save me some cake I said to my sister.

12. I sure hope we don't have any bad hurricanes this year

13. I'm going to Kimberly slumber party next Friday.

14. Our family is going to texas on vacation.

15. Somebody had better mind their own business.

16. My new stepmother speaks french.

17. Trahn want to play baseball.

18. as soon as I clean my room I'm going to watch television.

19. You'll love my new bedroom we painted it a really cool shade of green.

20. Each of my cats has their own bed.

Punctuation Practice #2
FEED THE MONKEY!

Mongo the monkey must climb down one step at a time to reach his beloved bananas, and he is one HUNGRY monkey. Find and correct the punctuation error in each sentence below. When you find the error and correct it, draw a line down from Mongo to the next step.

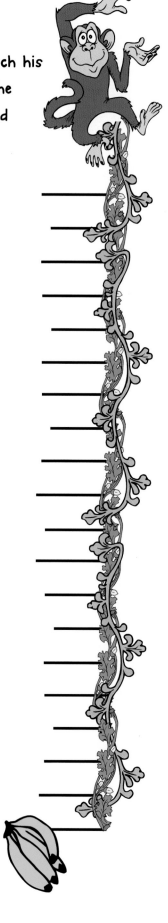

1. I don't feel so well I'm not going to school today.

2. the rest of the guys are coming over this afternoon.

3. I'm so excited we won the game.

4. My friends father is a rodeo cowboy.

5. The world's best baseball team.

6. I made chicken purlow for supper Mother said.

7. I dug a hole in the back yard with ryan and michelle.

8. Did you find anything.

9. I don't have no answers for you.

10. Ran quickly across the meadow.

11. Carley is on restriction until tuesday afternoon.

12. I'm sorry I yelled at you but I was mad

13. I borrowed Tanners basketball and forgot to give it back.

14. Are you ready yet I'm sick of waiting!

15. Jessica and Haley be on the cheerleading squad.

16. Thaddeus said I never know when you're kidding.

17. I don't no if I'm allergic to bee stings or not.

18. Carmine is moving to georgia next summer.

19. Did you enter the spelling bee!

20. Will julie be in the cafeteria for lunch today?

Punctuation Practice #3

PUNCTUATION SCAVENGER HUNT!

Give yourself ONE POINT for each error you find and correct.

Narrative Prompt: Write about a time when something funny happened.

Worms for Company!

I still laff to myself when i think about the time I fed Mrs. Sarten worms   i had made cupcakes and frosted them   I set them by the weendow to kool.   In the spring litle tiny green worms get on our weendow screens   I didnt no it but won of the worms got on the top of won of my cupcakes   My moms firend mrs Sarten came over. they were talk. My mom said katie why dont you serve sum of yore cupcakes I did Mrs. sarten said Mmm   These are good.   I looked at her   somehting on her cupcake moved.   My eyes opeend reel wide. it was one of the tiny green worms. It was inching along on the top of her cupcake   I was so shocked i almost fell off my chair. I couldnt think of inything to say   my mom and Mrs. Sarten didnt see the wurm   I clozed my eyes and tried to think of whut to say. when i opuned my eyes I looked at Mrs. Sarten. She was take a big bite. The worm was gone   I never told my mom   or Mrs. Sarten but it still make me laugh like a dug when I think about the time I fed mrs sarten litle crepy crawly things.

Expository Prompt: Write about a food you hate to eat.

Asparagus

Wouldn't yu no it? everytime I do to my aunt helens hous she makes dinner for our famly. Shes a good cook esept one thing. She always serves asparagus. now if youve never eaten it you mite not no what Im talkin about. Asparagus is a vegetable a green vegetable. They grow in little stalks and most peeple like them but i dont As a matter of fact I hate aparagus!!!!! My ant helen puts some on my plate. It has a sas on it to. My mom says Try some Oscar so I have to eet it you can't imagine how bad it tast. If someone puts asparagus on you plate run for your life

Conventions Crossword

Sizzling Words for Genius Writers

Answer key on page 211

ACROSS

1 Every sentence needs a _____ and a verb.

4 The words "everybody," "anybody," "anyone," "each," "neither," "nobody," "someone," and "a person" take _____ pronouns.

6 "My," "me," and "I" are all words we use when we are writing in the _____ person.

9 We use this mark when we want to show excitement. (2 words)

12 Use this mark to show when something belongs to someone.

13 Your subject and verb have to _____ with each other.

14 End an ordinary sentence with this.

15 This kind of noun needs a capital letter.

DOWN

2 Use this to start a sentence. (2 words)

3 Use the words "is" or "am" in the _____ tense.

5 End a sentence with this when you are asking something. (2 words)

7 The name of a city should start with this. (2 words)

8 Do this when you start a new paragraph.

10 Never use a _____ negative in a sentence.

11 Separate a list of nouns, adjectives, or adverbs by these.

Survival Skill Game

How to Play Survival Skill

1. Copy pages 130-131. Glue both pages to cardboard. Tape together on the back.

2. Make the spinner and game pieces according to the instructions below.

3. One person should be designated as the QUESTIONER. He asks the questions and checks for right answers. He may ask questions in any order from the Board Game Questions on pages 132 through 140.

4. Spin to see who goes first. First player to spin a 6 goes first. Play proceeds to that person's left.

5. When it is your turn, start by answering a Board Game Question. If you are correct, spin the spinner and move ahead. Wait for your next turn.

6. If you land on a square with an X, follow the instructions on the game board. Sometimes you will have to move back a few spaces. Sometimes you will move ahead. Read the instructions on the game board.

7. Follow the numbers all around the gameboard.

8. The first person to the finish line is the WINNER.

- -

Glue this sheet onto a half sheet of cardboard. Let dry. Cut out spinner, arrow, and 12 game pieces. Use a nail to punch a hole in the center of the spinner. Use a hole punch to punch a hole in the end of the arrow. Fasten the two together with a brad. Keep the brad loose enough so the spinner will still spin.

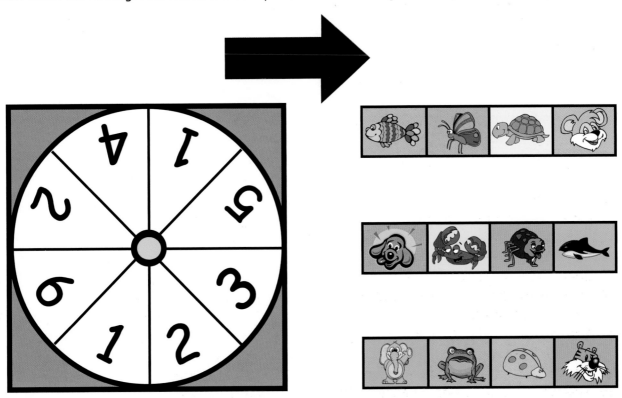

Survival Skill Game

START HERE

1
2
3
4
5
6 ✗

Oops! Forgot your compass. Spend one turn completely lost.

7
8
9
10
11
12
13 ✗

Too bad! You didn't bring enough water in your canteen. Spend one turn in the pond.

14
15
16

You left the food out, and it was found by a hungry bear. Roll a 1, 3, or a 5 and you can jump over the bear to square 47. Roll a 2, 4, or a 6, and you spend one turn in a tree!

46 ✗
45
44
43

47
48
49
50
51
52
53
54
55
56 ✗

P.U! You've startled a skunk! Spend one turn washing off the smell.

57
58
59
60
61
62
63 ✗

Good job of gathering firewood! Advance three spaces to 66!

64
65

Board Game Questions

Knowing the answers to these questions will help you on the grammar portion of FCAT Writes and improve your writing. You can use them with the board games on pp. 130-131 and pp. 142-143.

1. What word means to think quickly and creatively?
   Answer: brainstorming

2. How much time should you spend on planning before you begin to write for Florida Writes:
   A. 5 minutes, B. 10 minutes, or C. 15 minutes?
   Answer: A. 5 minutes

3. In what month is Florida Writes given?
   Answer: February

4. When writing has a beginning, a middle with many supportive details, and an ending, we say it has a feeling of _____.
   Answer: completeness

5. What does "focus" mean in our writing?
   Answer: to stay on topic

6. How many sheets of paper will you receive for planning and writing during Florida Writes?
   Answer: one for planning, two for writing

7. What do you call a first sentence that catches your reader's attention?
   Answer: a grabber (or a hook)

8. Which part of our writing should be short and to the point?
   Answer: the beginning

9. What do you call a verb you cannot picture?
   Answer: a weak verb

10. What word means to arrange your thoughts into a beginning, a middle, and an ending?
    Answer: organization

11. Which part of your writing should have vivid details, supporting reasons and examples, and possibly a mini-story?
    Answer: the middle

12. What type of ending tells the reader what you have learned or how your life has changed?
    Answer: a takeaway ending

13. What do you call a verb you can picture?
    Answer: a strong verb

14. What type of ending looks at "clues" and tells the reader the most important thought?
    Answer: a conclusion

15. What word means you have something to say, and you support it with vivid details?
    Answer: content

16. What word means all the writers' tricks that add beauty and maturity to your writing?
    Answer: creativity

17. True or False: You should not use a word in your writing unless you know how to spell it correctly.
    Answer: false

18. What do you call writing a few letters or drawing a quick picture to get your thoughts down on paper?
    Answer: jotting

19. Which is correct? A. *Jaden be in first grade.* Or, B. *Jaden is in first grade.*
    Answer: B. *Jaden is in first grade.*

20. What is a grabber supposed to do?
    Answer: grab the reader's attention

21. Which should always be capitalized? *mosquito, monster,* or *monday*
    Answer: Monday

22. Which is correct? A. *Sara brought her dog to school,* B. *Sara done bring her dog to school,*
    C. *Sara bring her dog to school*
    Answer: A. Sara brought her dog to school

23. When you read the words, "*tell about a time when,*" what is the prompt asking you to do?
    Answer: tell a story

24. Which kind of prompt asks you to explain something?
    Answer: an expository prompt

25. When you finish writing, what should you do until time is up?
    Answer: look for ways to revise and edit

26. Which paragraph is the most important one to indent?
    Answer: the first one

27. What can you do if you don't have a real story to tell?
    Answer: make one up

28. What do we call it when we make big changes to improve our writing?
    Answer: revising

29. What should you do if you forget to indent a paragraph?
    Answer: add the indentation sign

30. What do we call the following? brainstorming, mapping, webbing, listing, or storyboarding?
    Answer: prewriting or planning

31. Why is this sentence incorrect? *Each one of my friends is bringing their sleeping bag.*
    Answer: use *his* or *her* instead of *their*

32. If you know a sizzling word but you don't know how to spell it, what should you do?
    Answer: try to spell it like it sounds

33. What is the highest score you can get on Florida Writes?
    Answer: 6.0

34. What does it mean to "clarify" an idea?
    Answer: make it clearer or answer an unanswered question

35. What should you use to show that someone is talking?
    Answer: quotation marks

36. When you're telling a story, ideas, details, and events should be in what kind of order?
    Answer: logical order so they make sense (chronological order is also correct)

37. True or False: It's a good idea to end your writing piece with the words, "the end."
    Answer: false

38. What creativity skill means sound effects?
    Answer: onomatopoeia

...Board Game Questions

39. What do we call small changes we make to spelling, punctuation, and grammar after we have written?
    Answer: editing

40. Is this sentence correct or incorrect? *Someone didn't make their bed.*
    Answer: incorrect. Someone is singular. The sentence should read:
    Someone didn't make her bed. (or *his bed*)

41. Is this sentence correct or incorrect? *I didn't get no money for my allowance.*
    Answer: incorrect. There are two negatives in this sentence. The sentence should read:
    I didn't get any money for my allowance.

42. What are the two kinds of prompts you might get for Florida Writes?
    Answer: narrative or expository

43. What score would you get if you don't write on the topic?
    Answer: zero

44. What do we call the following phrases? *First of all, Let me explain, To begin with, Sometime later,*
    Here's another way to look at it
    Answer: transitional phrases

45. What does *creativity* mean in a writing piece?
    Answer: how beautifully you write and include descriptive writing, sizzling vocabulary, etc.

46. What kinds of sentence structures should you use?
    Answer: a variety of sentence structures

47. What do we call mature, interesting words that add beauty to our writing?
    Answer: sizzling vocabulary

48. What do you call a very short story that you include in a longer piece?
    Answer: a mini-story

49. Organized writing has a _____, a _____, and an _____.
    Answer: beginning, middle, ending

50. Should you refer to the prompt or copy it word for word?
    Answer: refer to the prompt

51. Which sentence is correct? *We're going Staci house to play.* Or *We're going to Staci's house to play.*
    Answer: *We're going to Staci's house to play.*

52. What is wrong with this passage? *I decorated my bike for the parade. I added streamers on the*
    handlebars. Then she pedaled off to join the other kids.
    Answer: The writer changed from first person (I) to third person (she)

53. What is wrong with this sentence? *Monique and Tammy two best friends.*
    Answer: There is no verb. The sentence should read,
    Monique and Tammy are two best friends.

54. What kind of end punctuation does this sentence need? *I just won the lottery.*
    Answer: an exclamation point

55. What should you use if you write the words, *finding nemo?*
    Answer: capital letters

56. What is a sentence fragment?
    Answer: a sentence without either a noun or an action word

57. What are the two times you can write sentence fragments?
    Answer: in dialogue or an aside

58. What is an aside?
    Answer: when you speak directly to the reader

59. Is this a sentence or a fragment? *"Mama, can I have another piece of corn bread?"*
    Answer: a sentence

60. Is this a sentence or a fragment? *Oh, yeah.*
    Answer: a fragment

61. Is this a sentence or a fragment? *My cousin's little baby brother.*
    Answer: a fragment

62. Is this a sentence or a fragment? *Yesterday we went to Kayla's dance recital.*
    Answer: a sentence

63. What is wrong with this sentence? *My cat had kittens she had a litter of four babies.*
    Answer: it's a run-on sentence

64. How do you spell *against?*
    Answer: a-g-a-i-n-s-t

65. How do you spell balloon?
    Answer: b-a-l-l-o-o-n

66. How do you spell college?
    Answer: c-o-l-l-e-g-e

67. What is a comparison between two unlikely things in order to make a point?
    Answer: a metaphor

68. What is an idiom?
    Answer: a colorful expression used to make a point

69. What do you call these types of phrases in your writing: *Did you like my story?*
    Do you have a story you want to tell me? I can't think of anything else to say.
    Answer: tacky expressions

70. What kind of verb is *went* in the following sentence?
    I went to Alberto's house after ball practice.
    Answer: a weak verb. A strong verb would be:
    I walked over to Alberto's house after ball practice. Or *I rode my bike over to Alberto's house.*

71. What word means to write with excitement and emotion?
    Answer: passion

72. What do we need to do with the following sentences: *Sam loves hamburgers. He loves big hamburgers.*
    He loves hamburgers with pickles and cheese. He loves juicy hamburgers.
    Answer: combine them into one sentence with all of the important words

73. What does *voice* mean?
    Answer: putting your personality down on paper, sounding like a real person is writing

74. Is it okay to have a short sentence every now and then or should all of our sentences be long?
    Answer: it's okay to have a few short sentences

...Board Game Questions

75. Is this prompt expository or narrative?
    Think of your favorite place to relax. Now explain why this place is your favorite.
    Answer: expository

76. What do you call drawing your thoughts in several boxes before you write?
    Answer: storyboarding

77. Should your storyboard pictures be simple or detailed?
    Answer: simple

78. If you are writing a letter to your pen pal, who is your *audience* and what kind of tone would you use?
    Answer: your audience is another kid and your tone would be friendly and kid-like

79. How should you group details in the middle of your writing?
    Answer: like-details should go together

80. True or False: In order to fill up the paper, it is a good idea to go on and on, even if it's not important.
    Answer: false

81. What is a "mind movie"?
    Answer: a vivid image your reader "sees" in his mind when he reads your writing

82. What kind of grabber is this?
    Picture this: You accidentally spill ink, permanent ink, on your mom's white bathroom rug!
    Answer: a scenario

83. What kind of grabber is this? *"Step away from the chocolate and no one will get hurt," I said.*
    Answer: dialogue

84. What kind of grabber is this? *Have you ever been up in a hot-air balloon, high above the ground?*
    Answer: a rhetorical question

85. The part of the sentence that tells the action is known as the _____.
    Answer: verb, action word, or predicate

86. The part of the sentence that tells who or what the sentence is about is known as the _____.
    Answer: subject

87. What does descriptive language include?
    Answer: adjectives, adverbs, word pictures, "mind movies," and specific words (any of these)

88. True or False: An expository prompt must be answered with five paragraphs.
    Answer: false

89. Periods, commas, question marks, and quotation marks are all forms of _____.
    Answer: punctuation

90. True or False: Every sentence should focus on the topic.
    Answer: true

91. *My favorite part, the next day, after that,* are all examples of _____.
    Answer: transitional phrases

92. Which is better, a transitional word or a transitional phrase?
    Answer: a transitional phrase

93. A _____ is when we compare two things using the words *like* or *as.*
    Answer: simile

...Board Game Questions

94. Should you revise or edit first?
    Answer: revise

95. What is the difference between revising and editing?
    Answer: revising means the big changes and editing means the little changes

96. When you're writing a rough draft, can you cross out words, add sizzling words, and make changes in the margins?
    Answer: absolutely (Florida Writes is a rough draft)

97. What usually gets you to a score of 4?
    Answer: having a beginning, a middle, and an ending that have content and completeness

98. What usually gets you to a score of 5 or 6?
    Answer: having great content AND a number of creativity skills that add entertainment and beauty

99. What do you call the following sentence? *Don't you just love spring break?*
    Answer: a rhetorical question

100. When you work with a partner, what are some things you can do to help your partner?
    Answer: listen attentively, give compliments, ask questions, make suggestions (any of these)

101. Which is an example of a simile? *He's as happy as a lark.* Or, *He is my best friend.*
    Answer: He's as happy as a lark.

102. Which sentence is more likely to "grab" your attention:
    A. *Last summer Duke, my golden retriever, surprised us all by digging up a skeleton in our neighbor's back yard.*
    B. *This is a story about Duke, my golden retriever.*
    Answer: the first sentence, A.

103. Which would best describe a substitute teacher who is angry with the class?
    A. *Mr. West was really, really, REALLY mad.*
    B. *Mr. West clenched his teeth and growled, "I'm calling the principal!"*
    Answer: the second sentence, B.

104. How do you spell the word *friends?*
    Answer: f-r-i-e-n-d-s

105. How do you spell the word *school?*
    Answer: s-c-h-o-o-l

106. What is missing in the following sentence:
    Ran for his life through the dark, creepy forest.
    Answer: the subject

107. An expository prompt asks you to _____.
    Answer: explain

108. True or False: You don't really need quotation marks when someone is talking.
    Answer: false

109. True or False: In a narrative, the events of your story should be in a logical order.
    Answer: true

110. True or False: If you don't like the prompt, you can write on whatever subject you choose.
    Answer: false (you must write to the prompt you are given)

111. Staying on topic is also called _____ on the topic.
    Answer: focusing

112. If you write a list of words in a series, what should you put between the words?
     Answer: commas

113. *Wham, fizz, achoo,* and *woof* are all examples of _____.
     Answer: onomatopoeia

114. When you first put your ideas down on paper, it's called a _____ draft.
     Answer: rough

115. The little marks that surround dialogue are known as _____.
     Answer: quotation marks

116. A more sizzling way to say the word *ran,* as in, *I ran to the playground,* would be
     I_____ to the playground.
     Answer: raced, zoomed, sprinted, zipped, tore off, galloped, bounded, etc. (any)

117. Listen to the following passage:
     Can you imagine clickety-clacking up a steep hill, hanging at the top for a second, and then zipping downhill at almost 50 miles an hour? Well, that's what happens when you ride the new Expedition Everest ride at Disney's Animal Kingdom. You speed through dark tunnels, go backwards, almost crash, and scream for dear life because you think you might die. Then, when the ride is over, you beg, "Can we go again?"
     The main idea is:
     A. You want to go again
     B. Animal Kingdom has a new ride
     C. The Expedition Everest ride is exciting, scary, and not-to-be-missed
     Answer: C

118. *Pistachio* is a sizzling color word in what color family?
     Answer: green

119. *Ruby* is a sizzling color word in what color family?
     Answer: red

120: *Raven* is a sizzling color word in what color family?
     Answer: black

121. *Amethyst* is a sizzling color word in what color family?
     Answer: purple

122. True or False: Neatness is more important than content and creativity.
     Answer: false

123. A writing piece needs to have a sense of: A. purpose B. voice C. completeness
     D. all of the above
     Answer: D. all of the above

124. Which sentence gets off topic?
     I'm getting contact lenses! I have to wear glasses because I'm nearsighted, but I hate wearing them. I lose my glasses all the time. Once I stepped on them in the dark and broke them. When I play sports I get sweaty and my glasses slip off my nose. I'm really good at soccer. So my mom said that when she gets paid she's going to buy me some contact lenses.
     Answer: I'm really good at soccer

125. True or False: The most important thing about a good writing piece is to have perfect spelling.
     Answer: false

126. True or False: It's better to try to spell the word *gargantuan* than to write the word *big* because it's easier to spell.
     Answer: true

127. If you were writing about spending the day at the park, which sentence would be the best grabber?
     A. *I love going to the park.* B. *My name is Mandi and I'm going to tell you why I love going to the park.* C. *There are at least 1,000 cool things to do at the park, and I've done 999 of them.*
     Answer: C

128. What should a writer look for in order to form a conclusion?
     Answer: "clues" of important information

129. What is our motto for scoring on Florida Writes?
     Answer: at least a four and maybe more

130. For writers, what does S.W.A.T. stand for?
     Answer: successful writers avoid tackiness

131. True or False: If you make mistakes while you are writing, just cross them out
     and keep going without stopping to erase.
     Answer: true

132. True or False: You should start writing as soon as you read the prompt.
     Answer: false (read it several times, think about it, then plan)

133. True or False: If you find you've left out a word you can write it above the line or in the margin.
     Answer: true

134. True or False: You have to write in cursive writing for Florida Writes.
     Answer: false

135. True or False: Punctuation and grammar should be correct most of the time.
     Answer: true

136. Is this sentence correct or incorrect?
     Fernando doesn't know nobody who can help him with his homework.
     Answer: incorrect (double negatives: *doesn't* and *nobody*)

137. True or False: You do not need a title when you are writing for Florida Writes.
     Answer: true

138. True or False: You should write with different kinds of beginnings for some of your sentences.
     Answer: true

139. What should you support your topic with?
     Answer: reasons, details, examples, quotes, a mini-story, etc.

140. What kinds of words are the following adjectives: *sticky, gooey, delicious*
     Answer: specific sensory words

141. If you accidentally burped out loud while the principal was visiting your class,
     what word describes how you might feel?
     Answer: embarrassed, humiliated, ashamed, upset, mortified (any like these)

142. If your teacher tells you that you have won an all-expense paid trip to Australia
     and you can bring your best friend, what word describes how you might feel?
     Answer: thrilled, excited, joyous, joyful, overjoyed, happy, glad, surprised (any like these)

143. When we add glitz, sizzle and "snap" to our writing, it can be said that our writing has a
     sense of _____.
     Answer: style

144. What is the subject and the verb in the following sentence?
     Last week I broke my arm.
     Answer: *I* is the subject, *broke* is the verb

...Board Game Questions

145. What do we call this phrase? *I'm all ears.*
     Answer: a metaphor

146. Is the following sentence correct or incorrect?
     Somebody had better mind her own business.
     Answer: correct (*somebody* and *her* are both singular)

147. When should you use an exclamation point?
     Answer: when you want to show excitement

148. True or False: You should use capital letters when you write the days of the week
     and the months of the year.
     Answer: true

149. What is wrong with the following sentence?
     Those chimpanzees at the zoo make me laugh you should see them make crazy monkey faces!
     Answer: a run-on sentence

150. What creativity skill is in the following sentence?
     Matt Cato is an accident waiting to happen.
     Answer: a metaphor

151. What are four of the nine kinds of grabbers you can use?
     Answer: scenario, voice, mystery, opinion, onomatopoeia, dialogue, global/specific statement,
     rhetorical question, humorous statement

152. What should a grabber do?
     Answer: a grabber should capture your reader's attention.

153. Spell Florida.
     Answer: capital F-l-o-r-i-d-a

154. How should you divide your time when you have 45 minutes to write?
     Answer: five minutes of planning, 25 minutes of writing, and ten minutes of revising

155. What is the weakest part of most writing?
     Answer: the ending

156. What is wrong with the following passage?
     I go to the dentist every year he cleans my teeth and looks for cavities.
     Answer: it is a run-on sentence

157. What error do you find in the following sentence?
     My art teacher, mrs. stevens, can draw like you wouldn't believe!
     Answer: Mrs. Stevens is a proper noun and should be capitalized

158. What should the beginning of a piece do for the reader?
     Answer: tell him what you are writing about (tell him the subject or the topic)

159. What two things does a narrative do?
     Answer: a narrative tells a story and shows the passing of time

160. What does a comparison do for your reader?
     Answer: a comparison helps your reader form a mental picture

161. True or False: The word Orlando is a proper noun.
     Answer: true

162. True or False: It is okay to cross out words and make changes on a rough draft.
     Answer: true

Race to the Finish Game

How to Play Race to the Finish

1. Copy pages 142-143. Cut on the dotted lines. Glue both pages to cardboard. Tape the pages together on the back so they form a gameboard.

2. Copy the car below. Glue the car to cardboard. Make sure to glue it and let it dry before you decorate it and cut it out.

3. Decorate your car-set with colored pens so that it looks like a big, bad, awesome race car! Use all your imagination and creativity.

4. Cut out your car-set.

5. Fold in half so you have two halves of a car. Fold out the bottom tabs so your car stands up. This looks so cool!

6. One person should be designated as the QUESTIONER. She asks the questions and checks for right answers. She may ask questions in any order from the Board Game Questions on pages 132 through 140.

7. Flip a coin to see who goes first. Take turns answering questions. For every correct question, advance one space. For every incorrect question, go back one space. The first person to the finish line is the WINNER.

Race to the Finish

How Many Points Can You Score?

START YOUR ENGINES!

31

32

33

34

START FINISH

30

29

28

27

26

25

1

2

3

4

5

6

© 2007 Melissa Forney www.melissaforney.com

RACE to the FINISH!

13 14 15 16 17 18

12 19

11 20

10 21

9 22

8 23

7 24

Using your Best Spelling

Spelling is another one of our editing skills that serves as a courtesy to our readers. Spelling is important, but you don't have to be the best speller to be a great writer.

Spelling is a code we learn so we can understand each other's writing.

My *new camera is phenomenal*.

Not all of your words must be spelled perfectly when you're writing a rough draft. We can try to write words we don't know how to spell by spelling them how they sound.

My *new camra is fenomenal*.

It's easy to figure out the words the writer wanted us to read.

It's okay to guess at words you don't know.

But, you do need to spell **most** of your words correctly, particularly easy, common words. If you want to use a real big, juicy word, don't be afraid to try to spell it how you think it should be spelled. Your reader will probably be able to figure out what you mean.

When you write the common, easy words, try to use your best spelling. Show your reader (and the person who is scoring your paper) that you've learned the words you should know for your grade level.

While you're practicing writing, you can look up words in your "Spelling List for Genius Writers" on pp. 146-152 of this book, in the dictionary, or on the word wall in your class. You can ask other kids or your teacher for occasional spelling help. Be ready to lend a hand to other writers when they ask for help, too.

Lots of kids in first and second grade are worried about spelling. They won't write a word if they don't know how to spell it. They think they have to be perfect! As a result, their writing stays babyish and simple.

They have a lot to learn about writing. Do we have to be perfect? No way!

The most important thing is to relax when you are writing. Spell the easy words you know. Go ahead and use the big, juicy words you want to use. Guess at the spelling or just jot down a few letters as you're writing your rough draft. Later, after you've finished writing, you can edit your paper and look up those words. Use every resource available to you to find the right way to spell the words you guess at: the dictionary, the thesaurus, the word wall, etc. Learn these words. Memorize several sizzling words that are your "dazzle words."

Dazzling Spelling Word Search

The more you work with words the better you know them. See if you can locate these impressive words in the word search grid below. Answers can go across, up, down, and diagonally. Give yourself 5 points for every answer you find!

```
R  L  R  Q  T  D  B  H  A  N  D  I  C  A  P  P  E  D  C
G  A  R  G  A  N  T  U  A  N  R  A  M  A  Z  E  D  Q  M
T  I  K  V  E  G  E  T  A  B  L  E  M  K  T  M  U  L  T
W  Q  M  P  D  Q  L  R  Q  J  Q  A  L  C  V  E  B  N  R
M  H  W  A  G  F  W  A  Y  U  G  M  E  C  S  C  E  N  R
N  R  E  W  G  T  M  X  D  I  I  P  V  T  C  D  M  B  F
W  R  D  W  K  I  H  K  C  I  S  C  I  H  I  C  Z  N  R
N  N  N  B  E  J  N  A  L  E  A  O  K  C  X  Q  T  L  C
K  M  E  I  M  T  L  A  R  W  N  T  C  L  R  J  G  H  W
N  O  S  L  B  N  L  S  T  B  N  A  O  Z  Y  D  O  T  T
O  N  D  L  A  L  I  T  K  I  E  B  K  R  Z  R  L  E  C
W  S  A  I  R  D  K  T  B  J  O  A  C  F  E  H  N  B  C
L  T  Y  O  R  Y  R  Q  N  F  A  N  U  O  D  O  V  I  R
E  R  J  N  A  M  N  K  T  D  R  F  G  T  H  X  T  N  T
D  O  C  A  S  Z  L  T  I  W  A  R  C  P  I  N  T  P  R
G  U  P  I  S  N  F  R  V  M  A  P  O  Q  A  F  L  K  Y
E  S  Y  R  T  J  O  W  O  P  N  L  L  G  B  R  U  F  W
R  M  Z  E  G  L  R  U  H  X  Y  B  I  R  V  C  P  L  K
C  Y  G  V  F  M  S  Y  C  X  W  G  F  Q  B  W  W  R  H
```

Answer Key on p. 211

DAZZLE DAZZLE DAZZLE

accident
amazed
beautiful
billionaire
choreography
disrespect
handicapped
gladiator
embarrass
famous
gigantic

gargantuan
imagination
knowledge
magical
monstrous
xylophone
Wednesday
vegetable
quickly
question
Florida

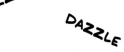

DAZZLE DAZZLE

A Spelling List for Genius Writers

A

a lot
able
about
above
accident
accuse
across
active
add
address
adjective
admit
adult
adverb
advice
afford
afraid
Africa
African-American
against
age
ago
ahead
aim
air
Alabama
Alaska
all right
alligator
allow
all-star
alone
along
aloud
alphabet
already
also
although
always
amaze
America
American
among
amount
an
anchor
and
angel
angle
animal
ankle
annoy
another

answer
ant
Antarctica
anything
apart
ape
appear
apple
apply
April
area
arena
argue
Arizona
Arkansas
arm
army
around
arrive
art
ash
Asia
ask
asked
Atlantic
athletic
attach
attack
August
aunt
Australia
author
auto
avenue
award
aware
away
awesome
awful

B

baboon
baby
baby-sit
back
backbone
bad
badge
bag
bagel
baggage
bait
bake

balance
bald
ball
ballet
balloon
ball-point
banana
bank
barn
barnyard
base
baseball
bass
bath
bathtub
batter
bawl
be
beach
beagle
bear
beard
beautiful
beauty
became
because
become
bed
bee
beef
been
began
beggar
begin
behave
behind
being
believe
bell
belly
below
bench
bend
beneath
berry
besides
best
better
between
beyond
bicycle
big
bike

bill
billion
billionaire
bird
bitter
blab
black
blackboard
blame
bleed
blink
blob
blood
blow-dried
blow-dry
blue
blush
board
boat
body
bogus
bold
bone
bony
book
bored
boring
born
bother
bottom
bowl
box
boxer
boy
brace
branch
brass
bread
breakfast
brief
bright
brighten
brilliant
bring
broccoli
broken
brother
brush
brutal
bubble
buckle
build
bull

bully
bumblebee
bumpy
bundle
burp
bury
business
butter
buy
buzz
by
bye-bye

C

cab
cabin
cake
calf
California
call
called
caller
calling
calm
camel
camera
can
can't
Canada
Canadian
canal
candle
cannot
canoe
cap
caption
captive
car
carbon
career
careful
carpenter
carpool
carrot
carry

cart	claim	conquer	December	display
cartoon	clam	constitution	decide	disrespect
cash	clang	consult	deck	distance
cashier	clap	control	decode	distant
cast	class	cool	decorate	ditch
casual	classic	corrupt	decrease	dive
cat	classmates	could	deep	dived
catalog	classy	count	deer	divorce
catch	clean	country	defrost	do
cave	cleanse	course	degrade	doctor
celebrate	clear	cow	degree	doe
cell	clicker	cowboy	deja vu	does
cemetery	climate	cowgirl	Delaware	dog
center	climb	crab	delete	doghouse
Central America	clip	crater	delicate	dollar
certain	clock	crib	deliver	dollhouse
chalk	close	crinkle	demonstrate	dolphin
chalkboard	cloth	crisscross	deny	donate
champ	clothes	cross	depart	donkey
change	club	crowd	deprive	doom
chapter	cluck	crude	deputy	door
charge	clue	curly	derby	dot
chart	clump	cursive	desk	double
chatter	clutter	cushion	desktop	doughnut
chauffeur	coarse	cut	despise	downhill
cheap	coat		details	dragon
check	cobweb	**D**	devote	dragonfly
cheek	cockroach	dad	dew	drain
cheerful	cocoa	daddy	dial	drama
cheese	coconut	daily	diary	drastic
cheeseburger	cocoon	dairy	dictator	drawback
cheesecake	coffee	damp	did	dress
chew	Coke	dance	die	dribble
chewing gum	cold	dandy	diet	drift
child	collar	danger	different	drop
children	college	dangerous	difficult	dry
chili	cologne	dare	digest	dryer
chimp	Colorado	daredevil	dim	duck
China	comb	daring	dinky	dull
chocolate	come	dark	dinner	dune
choice	comedian	darken	dinosaur	dunk
choir	comedy	darkness	diploma	duration
choke	comma	dash	direct	during
chomp	command	date	directions	duty
chop	commercial	daughter	dirty	dynamic
choreography	common	dawn	disappear	
chorus	communicate	day	disappoint	**E**
chosen	company	daydream	disaster	each
chuckle	complain	daylight	disconnect	eager
cinema	complete	daze	discount	eagle
circle	compliment	dazzle	discovery	ear
cities	computer	dead	discuss	earn
citizen	cone	deaf	dishonest	earth
citrus	confess	dear	dismiss	ease
city	Congress	death	disobedient	east
civilization	Connecticut	deathly	disobey	easy

eat
ebony
echo
edge
eel
eerie
effort
egg
ego
Egypt
eight
either
eject
elbow
elevator
elect
electric
eleven
elite
else
embarrass
emerald
emotion
empty
end
endless
endure
enforce
English
enjoy
enormous
enroll
entertain
envelope
equator
eraser
Europe
eve
even
evening
event
ever
every
everyone
everything
exactly
except
exchange
excite
exercise
exhale
expose
extreme
eye witness
eyeball
eyelash

F

face
fact
fail
fair
fairly
fall
false
family
famous
far
farm
farmer
fashion
fast
father
feather
February
federal
fee
feed
feel
feet
fellow
festival
fever
few
fiction
fiddle
field
fiery
file
filler
film
final
finalist
finally
finger
fire
first
firstborn
fish
fix
fixable
flag
flatter
flea
flee
flip
flirt
floor
Florida
florist
fly
folk

follow
follower
food
fool
foolish
foot
forbid
forever
forget
forgive
form
fort
fortress
forty
fossil
foul
four
fox
fractions
frame
frantic
free
freeze
Friday
friend
fright
from
fuel
full
fully
function
fund
fur
furniture
fussy
future
futuristic
fuzzy

G

gadget
gallon
gallop
game
gang
gap
garbage
garden
gardener
gargle
gas
gasp
gaze
Georgia
general
generic

generous
gentle
genuine
gerbil
germ
gesture
get
giant
gigantic
giggle
girl
give
given
glad
gladiator
glass
gleam
glob
globe
glow
glue
gnaw
go
goat
God
going
gold
gone
good
good-bye
gooey
goon
goose
gorilla
got
grade
graduate
grammar
grand
grandfather
grandma
grandmother
grandpa
grasp
grave
gravity
green
gremlin
grew
grief
grime
grip
gripe
grizzly
groovy
gross

group
grow
growl
grown
growth
grubby
grudge
gruff
guard
guidance
guide
gulp
gum
gumball
gurgle
guts
gutter

H

habit
hack
hag
hail
hair
haircut
half
hall
halt
hand
handicapped
handle
handstand
handy
handyman
hang
hangar
happen
happened
harbor
hard
harmony
harp
harvest
hassle
hate
hatred
haul
have
Hawaii
hawk
hay
haze
he
head
hear
heart

heartbroken
heavy
hectic
held
help
helper
helpful
helping
helpless
her
herbal
here
hers
herself
hesitate
high
highway
hilarious
him
himself
hip
Hispanic
history
hobby
hog
hold
Hollywood
home
honey
honor
hook
hothead
hour
how
however
howl
hug
huge
hum
human
humiliate
husband

I

I
I'll
ice
icicle
icy
Idaho
idea
ideal
idiot
if
igloo
ill

illegal
Illinois
illness
image
imagine
imagination
imitate
immature
impact
important
impress
in
inch
include
income
index
Indian
Indiana
indoor
industry
infant
infect
inflate
inhale
injury
ink
inn
insect
inside
instant
instead
instruct
instructor
insult
intense
international
into
involve
Iowa
iron
is
island
isn't
issue
it
it's
itchy
its
itself
ivy

J

jacket
jail
jam
January

jar
jealous
jeans
jeep
Jello
jelly
jerk
jet
jewel
jiffy
jingle
job
jogger
join
joke
jot
joy
joyful
judge
juice
juicy
July
jump
June
jungle
junk
jury
just
justice
jut

K

Kansas
keen
keep
keg
kennel
Kentucky
key
kid
kill
kind
kindergarten
kindness
king
kingdom
kiss
kit
kitchen
kite
kitten
kitty
knee
knife
knit
knives

knob
knock
knockout
know
knowledge
kung fu

L

label
labor
lace
lady
lake
lamb
lame
lamp
land
lane
language
lap
large
laser
last
late
later
laugh
laughter
lava
lawn
lay
lazy
lead
leader
leaf
leak
lean
leap
learn
learner
leash
least
leather
leave
leaves
ledge
left
leg
lemon
length
lens
less
let
let's
letter
level
liberty

lick
lid
lie
life
light
like
lime
line
lion
lip
list
listen
little
live
lives
living
load
loan
log
long
longer
look
loop
loose
lose
loss
lost
lot
loud
Louisiana
love
loved
low
lower
lowest
lucky
lunch
lung

M

mad
made
magic
magnet
mail
main
Maine
make
mall
man
many
map
March
Maryland
marine
mark

A Spelling List for Genius Writers   PAGE FIVE

mask	musk	ocean	paste	possible
Massachusetts	must	October	pastry	post
mat	my	odd	pat	pot
matter		of	patch	pow
may	**N**	off	path	powder
May	nail	office	pattern	power
me	name	often	pause	preach
mean	nap	oh	paws	present
meat	napkin	Ohio	peace	president
meet	nasty	okay	peach	pressure
melt	navy	Oklahoma	pear	pretty
memory	near	old	peek	print
men	Nebraska	on	pen	prison
menu	neck	once	pencil	private
meow	need	one	Pennsylvania	probably
mess	nephew	only	penny	problem
Mexico	nervous	open	people	prove
Mexican	nest	opera	pepper	pudding
Michigan	net	orange	perfect	pup
might	Nevada	orbit	perfume	puppy
mile	never	orchestra	perhaps	pure
milk	new	order	period	purr
mind	New Hampshire	Oregon	permit	push
mine	New Jersey	orphan	person	put
Minnesota	New Mexico	other	pet	
mint	New York	ouch!	photo	**Q**
minus	next	our	piano	quack
miss	nice	out	pick	quake
Mississippi	niece	outer space	pickup truck	quart
Missouri	night	outside	picture	quarter
mist	nine	oven	pie	queen
misty	no	over	piece	quest
mix	noise	owl	pig	question
mom	none	own	pillow	quick
Monday	noon	ox	pin	quickly
money	north	oyster	pizza	quiet
monster	North America	**P**	place	quit
Montana	North Carolina		plain	quite
mood	North Dakota	Pacific	plane	quiz
moon	nose	package	plant	
more	not	page	plaster	**R**
morning	note	pail	plastic	rabbit
most	nothing	pain	play	race
motel	notice	pair	plug	raft
mother	noun	pajamas	pocket	rags
mouse	November	pale	poem	raid
move	number	palm	poet	rail
movie	nurse	pan	poetry	rain
mow	nut	pancake	point	raisin
much	**O**	pants	polar	rake
mud		paper	pole	ram
muddy	oak	pardon	pony	ran
mule	oar	park	poor	rap
mummy	oat	part	pop	rat
munch	obey	party	popcorn	raw
muscle	occur	past	porch	react

150 Writing Superstars

A Spelling List for Genius Writers PAGE SIX

read
reading
real
really
record
red
reed
reel
refugee
refund
relax
remain
remember
remove
rent
repair
request
rescue
research
respect
rest
restaurant
retreat
review
Rhode Island
rice
rid
ride
right
ring
rip
ripe
risky
river
road
rob
rock
rod 'n reel
rode
role
roll
roof
room
roost
root
rose
rot
rotten
round
row
row boat
rude
rug
run
rung
runner

rust
rut

S

sack
sad
safe
said
sail
sale
same
sand
sat
Saturday
save
saw
say
scary
school
science
sea
season
second
secret
see
seed
seen
self
sell
sentence
September
set
seven
sew
shake
shall
shape
she
sheep
shelf
shine
ship
shirt
shoes
shop
short
should
show
shown
shut
sick
side
sight
sign
simple
since

sing
six
size
skate
ski
skin
skip
skunk
sky
slap
sleep
slip
slow
small
smell
snack
snake
snow
so
soap
sock
soft
some
someone
something
son
song
soon
sore
sound
south
South America
South Carolina
South Dakota
space
speak
special
spin
spot
spring
square
stack
stairs
stamp
stand
star
start
state
stay
step
stick
still
stink
stinky
stock
stood

stop
store
story
street
string
strong
student
such
suddenly
sum
summer
sun
Sunday
super
sure
surely
surf
surface
sweep
sweet
swim
system

T

table
tail
take
taken
tale
talk
tall
tan
tank
tap
tape
taste
tax
tea
teach
teacher
tear
teen
teeth
telephone
tell
temper
ten
Tennessee
Texas
than
thank
thankful
Thanksgiving
that
that's
the

their
them
themselves
then
there
these
they
thick
thing
third
thirty
this
though
thought
three
threw
through
throw
thumb
Thursday
tiger
time
tiny
tip
to
today
toe
together
too
took
tool
tooth
top
touch
toward
town
toy
trade
trap
travel
treat
tree
truck
true
truth
try
tube
Tuesday
tug
turn
turned
turtle
twenty
twice
two
type

U
ugly
under
understand
until
United States
up
us
use
useful
useless
usually
Utah
utter

V
valentine
van
vase
vast
vat
vegetable
vent
verb
Vermont
very
vet
video
view
violin
Virginia
visit
visitor
vocal
voice
vowel

W
wait
wake
walk
walked
want
war
warm
was
wash
Washington
Washington, D.C.
watch
water
wave
wax
way
we

weak
wear
weather
web
Wednesday
weed
week
weight
well
went
were
West Virginia
wet
whale
wheel
when
where
whether
which
while
whip
whisper
white
who
whole
why
wide
wife
wiggle
wild
will
wind
wink
winter
wire
Wisconsin
wise
witch
with
within
without
wolf
woman
women
wonder
wood
word
work
world
worm
worse
worn
would
write
wrong
Wyoming

X
Xerox
x-ray
xylophone

Y
yard
yawn
year
yield
yell
yellow
yes
yesterday
you
you're
young
your
yourself
yo-yo
yummy

Z
zap
zebra
zero
zigzag
zillion
zing
zip
zipper
zone
zoo
zoom

Words I frequently use:

_____
_____
_____
_____
_____
_____
_____
_____
_____
_____
_____
_____
_____
_____
_____
_____
_____
_____
_____
_____
_____
_____
_____
_____
_____
_____
_____
_____
_____

Three Parts of Writing you Need to Score Well

| Details |
| Examples |
| Reasons |

CONTENT

Having plenty of content is the foundation of your writing.

Content means what you have to say.

It's the base of everything else you add to your writing. Without good content, your writing would be empty, hollow, and flimsy.

Picture a fancy cake you've seen at a birthday party or a wedding. The layers of cake form the foundation. The baker builds the cake by stacking one layer on top of the next. The basic cake might be delicious, but it's not yet a thing of beauty. The pastry chef will have to add his creative and decorative touches.
And, just like a baker, a writer builds his writing on an impressive foundation.

Writing must have a solid foundation of content, including details, examples, and reasons.

CREATIVITY

The icing is usually the most impressive part of a magnificent cake. This sweet, delicious, visible layer is where the baker can use all of his skills to impress guests who will eat the cake. Pastry chefs use swirlies, squiggles, roses, piping, curleyques, and an amazing assortment of bright candies and sprinkles to decorate their creations.

Isn't that just like when we write something for our readers?

After a good foundation of content, a writer pulls out all of his creativity skills to enhance his writing and impress his readers.

The creativity skills we writers add to our writing "decorate" our writing just like a beautifully iced cake.

Creativity means to add layers of beauty, sparkle, and wonder to writing.

CONVENTIONS

What could be worse than having a world-class, splendidly decorated layer cake and no way to eat it? If you were at a fancy dinner or at a wedding reception, you probably wouldn't just break off a huge chunk of cake and start eating it with your hands! You'd need a knife to slice it and a plate and a fork so you could eat it.

Conventions mean spelling, handwriting, grammar, and punctuation.

Handwriting, spelling, grammar, and punctuation don't really have anything to do with the content and creativity of a piece of writing, but without them the reader would not be able to read the story or information the author wants to say.

Writing conventions make our writing easy to read.

"Bulk Up" your Writing With Weight!

Great writing deserves its rewards! Keep a "weight chart" of your writing as you grow and progress as a writer. This helps you to be aware of the content, creativity, and convention skills you add to your writing. Just like a fine athlete adding to his training, add to your own growth as a writer one skill at a time.

Instructions for Making Weight Sheet

For this project you'll need:

scissors   color copies
stiff paper   three velcro dot sets cut in half = six sets

1. Copy page 155 on stiff paper.

2. Copy the weights below on stiff paper. Cut out each weight. Take your time.

3. Cut the three velcro dot sets in half so that you have six velcro dot sets.

4. Stick one velcro dot piece to the back of each weight you cut out.

5. Stick the other halves of the velcro dot sets to the sides of the barbell.

6. Add on "weight" as you add layers of content, creativity, and conventions to your writing. You'll add beauty and maturity, too.

How much weight does your writing have?

velcro
velcro
velcro

velcro
velcro
velcro

CONTENT

250 lbs. Beginning + Middle + Ending
250 lbs. 6-8 Vivid Supporting Details
250 lbs. 9-15 Vivid Supporting Details
250 lbs. Every Sentence Focuses on Topic

CREATIVITY

250 lbs. 3-5 Creativity Skills
250 lbs. 6-7 Creativity Skills
250 lbs. 8-10 Creativity Skills
250 lbs. Descriptive Writing

CONVENTIONS

250 lbs. Capital Letters
250 lbs. End Punctuation
250 lbs. Complete Sentences
250 lbs. Spelling

What Does a Narrative Four Look Like?

Since our motto is, "At least a four and maybe more," let's compare a four, a five, and a six. Will there be many differences? We'll start with a narrative prompt, one that TELLS A STORY and shows the passing of time, and show it written as a four, a five, and a six.

Narrative Prompt: Everyone has had an accident or gotten hurt sometime. Think of a time you got hurt. Now write about the time you got hurt.

I will never forget the time I had the most horrible bicycle accident in the world. I'd like to forget it, but it was a nightmare. Nightmares stay with you forever!

For my eighth birthday I got a brand new bike. Man, was it cool! That thing was so awesome. It was silver and green with racing pedals and trick handlebars. I thought it was the most beautiful bike in the world. My mom and dad gave it to me. I started riding it everywhere. I wanted all of my friends to watch me ride and see how beautiful the bike was. My dad warned me to be careful. I was careful for a while. But then I started doing more and more tricks. I started doing cool wheelies & handstands on the handlebars. It was amazing. One minute I'd be riding down the street, and the next minute I'd be popping up in the air doing a handstand. I fell a few times, but nothing serious.

Then one day I was down the street from where I live. My friends were with me and we were all doing tricks on our bikes. I told them to watch and I did a handstand on my handlebars. I didn't see that I was headed for a concrete bar thingy that was on the ground in front of me. My bike crashed and I went flying. I landed on my face. I looked like one big scab. I should have listened to my dad but I was having too much fun.

Next time I'll be more careful, but my bike is still cool.

This writer had a GREAT beginning. I could hardly wait to read about the accident. He included some good details in the middle, but when he got to the accident part, he cut it too short. He left out the details we wanted to hear about most! Even though the writing is pretty good, his lack of details limits him to a four.

What Does a Narrative Five Look Like?

The last writer got a four. But how can we boost our score even higher? This next writer is writing to the SAME PROMPT. Let's see what improvements he makes that would earn him a five instead of a four.

Narrative Prompt: Everyone has had an accident or gotten hurt sometime. Think of a time you got hurt. Now write about the time you got hurt.

"Crash!!!!!" That's the sound the bookshelves in our family room made when they ripped off the wall and thundered down on my head. The worst accident I ever had happened last summer when my cousin Delina was visiting.

Delina and I love to play together. We are like best friends even though we are cousins. One afternoon we were bored because we had to play inside all day. There was a terrible thunderstorm going on outside. We were watching television when all of a sudden lightning flashed and thunder crashed. The television went out and all of the lights went out, too.

Delina and I wondered what to do to keep ourselves from going crazy with boredom. First we got flashlights and started shining them all around. I had a flashlight that you wear on your head. It looked like one that climbers wear when they climb in caves, so I had an idea that would make Delina laugh. Our family room has tall bookshelves that go almost up to the ceiling. They're nailed to the wall and have about a thousand books on them. I got Delina's attention and said, "Watch this!" I started climbing up the bookcase like it was the inside wall of a cave. I used my hands and feet to pull myself up to the top. I finally turned around to see if she was watching. Just then I heard a loud "crack!" The bookcase was coming off the wall.

The shelf my foot was on came apart. Books flew everywhere. I tried to jump away, but I was up too high. When the bookshelf crashed to the floor my arm was sticking through the opening and it got broken in two places. I scraped my side and I had a huge bruise on my head. I also sprained my ankle. The books knocked Delina to the ground, too.

The next thing I knew, my mom came running into the room. Delina and I were both crying and scared. My mom at first thought I might have died. I didn't know my arm was broken but it hurt like crazy.

That's the last time I will ever climb on a bookshelf, believe me, no matter how bored I get.

This piece is quite good. Notice the strong verbs, dialogue, and onomatopoeia. With just a few more creativity skills and a stronger ending this would definitely have been a six.

What Does a Narrative Six Look Like?

We've saved the best for last. Let's see how the writer of the SAME PROMPT earned this six. By examining an "expert," maybe we'll become experts ourselves.

Narrative Prompt: Everyone has had an accident or gotten hurt sometime. Think of a time you got hurt. Now write about the time you got hurt.

Who would think that a little fishing hook could do so much damage! Last summer I had a traumatic experience that still makes me cringe when I think about it. My dad likes to call it the "Great Fish Hook Caper," but I call it "Matt's Day of Horror." As I begin my story, you better fasten your seatbelts. You might never hear another story like this again.

Here's the setting: I was fishing on Burke's Pier with my dad. That's a concrete pier that juts out onto the Mylora River. There were several other families fishing and a few old people sitting in lawn chairs. Now, I usually use a cane pole. That's the kind with the line that you just drop in the water. But this day I begged, "Dad, let me use the rod and reel." I had been practicing my casting in our back yard. I was pretty good, too. My dad said, "Okay, but be careful. Watch out for people. Always look behind you." I wanted to make a perfect cast and catch a huge fish!

The first few times I cast out my line things went well. I was careful like my dad asked. But the problem was that I wasn't catching anything. Other people on the pier were catching fish left and right, but when I reeled my line in...NOTHING. I was getting mad about it, so I forgot to be careful. I reached back to make the biggest cast ever. I placed my finger on the line. I whipped the rod with all of my might and released my finger at the same time. It was supposed to fly right up over my head, but instead, something went wrong. I tugged hard on the line and that's when I heard an ear-splitting scream. "AAAIIee!!!" I turned around and to my horror,

I saw that my hook was stuck in the lady on the other side of the bridge. She was bending over getting bait out of her bait bucket, and my hook snagged her right in the back of her shorts. Her husband turned to help her, but I was still pulling on the line. Just as he bent down, the hook ripped loose. It flew out and caught the edge of his fishing hat right by his eye and yanked the hat up in the air. I knew I was in bad trouble, and as it came sailing toward me, I reached up and tried to grab it out of the air. As I did, the barb end of the hook got stuck in my thumb. My dad had to cut the end of the barb off with wire cutters. I bled all over the man's hat. I had to apologize to him and his wife because they were MAD! I mean, the man was as hot as a firecracker. When I said I was sorry, I was so nervous and my finger hurt so bad I started crying. The man finally said, "Okay. It was just an accident." My dad just shook his head and gave me "the look."

I learned my lesson the hard way. Listen to your dad. If I had been more careful, we might have had "Matt's Great Fishing Day" instead of "Matt's Unforgettable Day of Horrors."

Now here's the real deal: a true 6.0. When we read this piece we can see the clear beginning, middle, and ending. This piece also gives us a feeling of completeness, lots of supporting details, tons of creativity, and great writer's tricks! There's no question: it's a six. With practice, you can write on this level, too. At least a four and...maybe more!

What Does an Expository Four Look Like?

Now let's look at an expository prompt, one that asks us to EXPLAIN and support our explanation with reasons and details.

Expository Prompt: Everyone needs to be healthy. Think of some things you should do to have a healthy life. Now write about how to have a healthy life.

Being healthy is a good thing. When you're not sick you have a better life and you have more fun. There are many things you can do to stay healthy.

Your body needs good food. You should eat lots of fruits and vegetables. Don't eat things that have a lot of fat in them. Cookies and greasy fries are fattening. Food gives you energy so you need to eat three good meals every day. Macaroni and cheese, green beans, salad, and applesauce would be a good meal because it has stuff from each of the food groups. Oh, be sure to eat healthy snacks, too.

You need exercise every day to be healthy. Exercise means running around and playing and riding your bike. Exercise keeps you from getting fat because it burns up calories. When you exercise, you develop muscle instead of fat. Don't sit in front of the TV all the time. There are some other things you can do to stay well. Don't smoke. Smoking causes cancer. Get plenty of sleep. Brush your teeth and take vitamins every day.

Taking care of yourself is important to keep from getting sick. I want to be healthy and have a good life, so I'm going to follow this advice.

Did you notice there is a beginning, a middle, and an ending? The writer supported the main idea with details you can "picture" in your mind. In order to get a higher score, however, she needs some more CREATIVITY SKILLS that would razzle dazzle the reader. Creativity rocks! Creativity can also raise your score.

What Does an Expository Five Look Like?

How can we bump that score higher than a four? Maybe if we compare this piece to the previous one we'll find out.

Expository Prompt: Everyone needs to be healthy. Think of some things you should do to have a healthy life. Now write about how to have a healthy life.

One of the most important things we can do is to stay healthy. Having a lot of money, or the best job in the world, or the fastest car is nothing compared to good health. Just ask a person who is sick all the time if you don't believe me.

Imagine what it would be like if you didn't have your health. You would not be able to play sports or go to the beach unless you had someone to help you and had an oxygen tank or a wheelchair.

One of the first things you can do to keep from getting sick is to get plenty of sleep. Our bodies need to rest. When my mom used to say, "Jeremy, time for bed," I did not want to go to sleep. But now I do. I stretch out in my comfortable bed and get 8 hours of sleep, so I'll feel supersonic in the morning.

You need to keep your body clean. Think about it. If you're dirty, germs and bacteria can move in and snack on you like you're a meal. Then you'll get all kinds of diseases. So keep yourself as clean as a whistle from head to toe. Oh, and don't forget your teeth. No one can have perfect health with a mouth full of rotten teeth.

How can you be healthy if you don't eat right? Make sure you eat a good breakfast every morning. Pack good stuff for your lunch like a ham sandwich, a scrumptious peach, some raisins, and milk. Try to eat a delicious meal at suppertime, and chew your food so you don't swallow and choke.

Think of being healthy as your responsibility. Take care of your body and you'll be able to do all of the things you want to do (well, most of them). Trust me. You won't be sorry if you treat your body like it's a valuable treasure.

Wow! Not only does the writer have a beginning, middle, and ending and supporting details you can picture, but there are noticeable CREATIVITY SKILLS. Did you spot dialogue, transitional phrases, sizzling vocabulary, a simile, metaphor, and voice?

What Does an Expository Six Look Like?

Yabba-dabba-doo! If you know what makes a four, a five, and a six, you can pretty much choose the score you want to receive. Just use plenty of CONTENT and CREATIVITY. Include the writers' tricks and skills that are sure to impress your reader. Let's drop in on another writer writing to the same prompt as the two we've already read. Since she ends up with a six, let's see if we can figure out how she does it.

Expository Prompt: Everyone needs to be healthy. Think of some things you should do to have a healthy life. Now write about how to have a healthy life.

There are thousands of sick, unhealthy people in this world. Being healthy is a special gift that allows us to enjoy the good things in life. Do you want to go to college? Would you like to play sports and be active? Can you imagine how cool it would be to travel all around the world seeing everything there is to see? Well, you can't do these things if you don't have good health. It's just that simple.

Your body is like a machine that requires fuel to make it run. Just like you put gas in a car, you have to put gas (food and water) in your body. You need delicious, scrumptious balanced meals and pure clean water every single day. Stay away from too much ice cream, potato chips, pizza, and junk food because they can make you fat and slow. That's why they call them "junk food," because they aren't the best foods for you. Eat healthy snacks like pretzels, celery sticks, carrots, jello, and yogurt.

Stay away from cigarettes. People who smoke smell like chimneys, and their teeth turn yellow and ugly. But the real reason not to smoke is because it causes CANCER. Yes, that terrible disease is caused by smoking. And people die from cancer every day, so don't even start to smoke so you won't get addicted and have a dreaded disease.

Another good way to stay healthy is to go to the doctor for regular visits. The doctor can give you a checkup and a physical to see if you are sick in any way. He can take your blood pressure and weigh you and ask you if you are having any symptoms. If you are, he will give you pills and medicine that can help you get well. I used to be afraid of going to the doctor because I was scared he would give me a shot. But last year I was very sick with strep throat and had to miss school and stay on the sofa. My throat hurt so bad I thought I would die! I went to the doctor and he did give me a shot, but I hardly felt it, and in less than two days I was well. Going to the doctor is definitely worth it.

Some of the best ways to keep healthy are really easy. You should get some kind of exercise every day, like riding your bike or swimming or walking in your neighborhood. Exercise builds up your strength and keeps you from being a couch potato. You can also stay healthy by keeping your body clean. Wash your hands after you go to the bathroom and especially before you eat. When your mom says, "Brush your teeth," do it. Take a bath and wash your hair, and put on clean clothes when you get up in the morning. Believe me, if you don't, you'll have germs and you'll stink and no one will want to be around you.

Learn how to keep healthy and stay that way. Then you can have a great life and enjoy all of the outstanding things there are to do in life. You only have one body. Don't abuse it!

Terrific! This piece is loaded with CONTENT you can picture, CREATIVITY SKILLS that add sparkle and maturity, and a fantastic beginning, middle, and ending. Compare this writer's expository piece with two previous ones, and you'll see what a true six looks like.

As a writer, you can "choose" the score you will get. It's not just a random thing. Pay attention to the qualities of a four, five, and a six. Make a list in your mind of skills you want to demonstrate in your own writing to get the highest score possible.

The Easy Way to Score

Scoring your writing doesn't have to give you the willy-nillies or "brain pain." There's actually a simple way to find your score. Now, it's my own Melissa-Forney-Way-To-Score, but I think you'll find that we'll arrive at the same score as the "official" way, and it's a thousand times easier for kids.

First of all, let's think of the six-point Florida Writes rubric scores in terms we can understand:

good scores
⭐ 6 = OUTSTANDING
⭐ 5 = Very Good
⭐ 4 = Good
3 = Okay
2 = Not Too Good
1 = Poor
O = Disastrous (nothing written on topic)

Now how do you apply these scores to your paper?

First, read your writing piece for pure enjoyment. Just listen to how it sounds. Now read it again carefully. **This time, look for FORMAT. The format we are looking for is beginning, middle, and ending.**

Ask yourself these three questions:

1. Does this piece have a beginning that is to the point, introducing us to the topic?
   If the answer is YES, give yourself ONE POINT.
2. Does this piece have a middle that tells a story or gives us details and reasons?
   If the answer is YES, give yourself ONE POINT.
3. Does this piece have an ending that is either a takeaway ending or a conclusion?
   If the answer is YES, give yourself ONE POINT.

So far you have a score of 3 if your paper has a complete beginning, middle, and an ending.

The next thing you'll look for is CONTENT. Content means that you have something to say. The middle is where we tell a complete story (narrative) or support the topic with reasons and details (expository).

For a narrative, ask yourself this question:

Does the middle tell a complete story with many details my reader can visualize?

For an expository piece, ask yourself this question:

Is the middle filled with details, details that go together, and details that explain and support the topic?

...The Easy Way to Score

If the answer is YES to either of these questions, give yourself ONE POINT.

So far you have a score of 4 if your paper is in the right FORMAT and has CONTENT.

Now it's time for you to look for CREATIVITY. Creativity means how beautifully you have expressed your story, ideas, and explanations.

Ask yourself this question:

Are there **at least** four or five successful CREATIVITY SKILLS I can point to that helped make my writing mature and entertaining for my reader?

If the answer is YES, give yourself ONE POINT.

So far you have a score of 5 if your paper is in the right FORMAT, and has CONTENT and CREATIVITY.

If you've gotten to a 5, you're flying high! Now it's time to ask yourself this important question:

Is this paper OUTSTANDING?

If the answer is YES, give yourself ONE POINT.

So far you have a score of 6!
Is there more? Aren't we finished? Not yet.

No matter what your final score, ask yourself this vital question:

Did I use readable handwriting, capital letters, periods, grammar, and correct spelling **MOST** of the time? (your teacher might have to help you with this one)

If the answer is YES, do not deduct anything from your score.
If the answer is NO, **DEDUCT** ONE POINT from your final score.

With a little practice, you'll figure out scoring in no time! As a matter of fact, we're going to practice scoring on some real papers so you'll get the hang of it.
Just remember these tips:

> A zero means you didn't write anything OR you didn't write anything on topic. You've got to write to the prompt and stay on the topic!

> 4, 5, and 6 are all good scores! You don't have to have a 6 to have a GOOD score.

Scoring Writing Sample #1

Let's practice scoring on a real writing sample. This narrative piece was written by a 4th grade Florida kid. Read it carefully. Look for format, content, and creativity. What score would you give it? Compare your score to mine.

Narrative Prompt: Write about a time you got into trouble.

The Worst Halloween Ever!!!

I am going to tell you about the worst Halloween ever!

Let me begin. My name is Ryan*. I'm the main character. My Halloween was the worst because I didn't trick o' treat! I know it sounds bad. But it gets worse! Because J. Dunworth (my exfriend!) stole a book and let me have it!

I was there and didn't tell him to stop. He let me have the book at recess to keep. When I got home I showed my mom the book. I told her my friend gave it to me. Then she questioned me.

I lied. She found out though. She has a power to know when you're lying or not. In the end I told her the truth. I was grounded from Halloween and a party my friend had! I was mad at myself and at J. Dunworth. I wished I was in Mrs. Groban's class. And, that I had never met the little rascal. Oh yeah, I was also grounded for the weekend!

On Halloween I weeped in my room. I was bursting out in tears. I cried my heart out. Thinking about what I did wrong. I began to pray to God. When I was done I felt bad. I feel bad this very moment. I'm giving him his book back.

We had pizza that night. Which is my favorite. I told my mom I was sorry. I even wrote her a letter. She said I was still grounded and couldn't trick o' treat.

I began to cry thinking of all the candy the kids on the bus would have, and me with nothing, not even a wrapper. I've learned my lesson. If you do something bad you will get caught.

Also, if you lie it'll make it worse. You should never lie to your parents treat them with respect and dignity! They will love you more than anyone else will.

If it wasn't for them you wouldn't be born! Be thankful for what you have. Don't want something so bad you'll take it.

*all names changed

Score for Writing Sample #1:   The Worst Halloween Ever   (narrative)

Category	Questions	Answers	Points
FORMAT	Does this piece have a beginning that is to the point, introducing us to the topic?	yes	1
	Does this piece have a middle that tells a story or explains details and reasons?	yes	1
	Does this piece have an ending?	yes	1
CONTENT	Does the middle tell a complete story or explain the topic fully with details the reader can visualize?	yes	1
CREATIVITY	Are there **at least** four or five successful CREATIVITY SKILLS I can point to that helped make the writing mature and entertaining for the reader?	no	-
MODEL	Is this paper OUTSTANDING?	no	-
CONVENTIONS	Did the writer have readable handwriting, capital letters, periods, grammar, and correct spelling MOST of the time?	yes	-

SCORE   4

Strengths:

The beginning grabbed my attention. This kid has great voice and passion! He also included some terrific details in the middle. Nice takeaway ending. I liked his creative transitional phrases. Notice his use of sentence variety. Way to go!

Weaknesses:

Although this story was enjoyable to read, there just weren't enough creativity skills in the middle to boost his score up to a 5 or a 6. He could have added dialogue, similes, etc.

Scorer's Comments:

I loved this story! Ryan wrote a funny, touching narrative, one we could all relate to.

Scoring Writing Sample #2

Here is an expository writing sample written by a 4th grade girl right here in Florida. Read it carefully. Then practice scoring. Compare your score and comments to mine.

Expository Prompt: Write about something you're good at.

Gymnastics

Some people are good at cooking, some people are good at pottery, but I'm great at gymnastics!

When I do gymnastics I feel that I'm free like a bird soaring millions of miles high in the sky! I taught myself how to do all of my own gymnastics except my cartwheel. I was in Tumbleweeds Gymnastics for a little over a month. All I learned to do there was a cartwheel. I'm right now on advanced level because I can go from a standing position to a back-bend. I hope I get to Juniors level soon. Gymnastics is everything to me! How it lifts my spirits when I'm down, or cries for me when I feel like crying, and is there for me when I need mending in my soul

Gymnastics I couldn't live without. Gymnastics makes me feel like putting wings on my back and fluttering up to the heavens above us. How you just close your eyes and get that upside down feeling for a millisecond then reality takes over. Within that millisecond it feels as if you have reality within the palm of your hand, but when you open your eyes again it all disappears into thin air. When I don't do gymnastics I feel empty and lonely like I'm the only person on planet earth who's alive and breathing, it's completely and totally horrific and terrifying. I can't stand the temptation going on in my mind, the irritable voices, the horrible, maniacal, laughing, the evil thoughts NO! NO! NO! NO! NO! NO!

Gymnastics is everything and I learn an important lesson from it. Stay fit and do it as much as I can. I can remember the first time I did a cartwheel....

My mom and I were sitting in the front yard watching the clouds when I got up and did a roll then a cartwheel it wasn't a very good one though.....

I love gymnastics and the most important thing is that's it's fun for me and maybe to you, too.

Score for Writing Sample #2:   Gymnastics   (expository)

Category	Questions	Answers	Points
FORMAT	Does this piece have a beginning that is to the point, introducing us to the topic?	yes	1
	Does this piece have a middle that tells a story or explains details and reasons?	yes	1
	Does this piece have an ending?	yes	1
CONTENT	Does the middle tell a complete story or explain the topic fully with details the reader can visualize?	yes	1
CREATIVITY	Are there **at least** four or five successful CREATIVITY SKILLS I can point to that helped make the writing mature and entertaining for the reader?	yes	5
MODEL	Is this paper OUTSTANDING?	no	-
CONVENTIONS	Did the writer have readable handwriting, capital letters, periods, grammar, and correct spelling MOST of the time?	yes	-

5   SCORE   5

Strengths:

What passion! This writer is not afraid to tell us the depths of her feelings. I love that about this piece. She writes with specific details that paint word pictures for me. Beautiful images! Lovely sentences!

Weaknesses:

I know she was trying to be creative, but the part about the evil voices just didn't fit the rest of this piece. I felt that when she got to the end of the third paragraph she started rambling. She ended the piece and then started up again, which was a bit confusing.

Scorer's Comments:

I think careful planning would have helped this writer give more specific details in the middle and write a more appropriate ending. This writer has a masterful command of images, and she could easily get a six with just a few small improvements. Great job!

Scoring Writing Sample #3

Here is an expository writing sample written by a 4th grade boy who calls Florida his home state. Read it carefully. Then practice scoring. Compare your score and comments to the ones I wrote.

Expository Prompt: Think of someone who is special to you. Now explain why they are special to you.

My Family

The ones That are special To me are my family. My family is good To me Through aloT. They are so good To me. I love my family so much. I have a greaT family. They are so good To me. My mom, dad, broTher, and sisTer are all good To me. I love my family very, very much because They are so good To me.

Score for Writing Sample #3:   My Family   (expository)

Category	Questions	Answers	Points
FORMAT	Does this piece have a beginning that is to the point, introducing us to the topic?	yes	1
	Does this piece have a middle that tells a story or explains details and reasons?	no	-
	Does this piece have an ending?	no	-
CONTENT	Does the middle tell a complete story or explain the topic fully with details the reader can visualize?	no	-
CREATIVITY	Are there **at least** four or five successful CREATIVITY SKILLS I can point to that helped make the writing mature and entertaining for the reader?	no	-
MODEL	Is this paper OUTSTANDING?	no	-
CONVENTIONS	Did the writer have readable handwriting, capital letters, periods, grammar, and correct spelling MOST of the time?	yes	-

SCORE __1__

Strengths:
   This writer gets right to the point.

Weaknesses:
   We can all see the problem here. This writer doesn't have a plan. There are no details to back up his beginning. I think he might have gotten a case of "brain freeze," and we all know what THAT is like!
   There is no way for us to have a "mind movie" of this kid's family because we need more specific details.

Scorer's Comments:
   This writer is a neat kid. His teacher told me so herself! If he were my student I'd say, "Don't be too hard on yourself. Just go back to the drawing board, and give us the juicy details about your family. Does your brother help you clean your room? Does your mom cook your favorite meals? Does your sister cheer for you at the soccer game? And what about Dad? Does he help you with your homework? Give us details!"

Scoring Writing Sample #4

Here's a kid who wanted to take you on a wild and scary adventure. Read his piece carefully. Practice scoring with your classmates. Compare your comments and score to mine.

Narrative Prompt: Write about a time something exciting happened to you.

My Trip to the Ocean

"Is that everything?" I yelled to my dad as I placed a bunch of ripe bananas in the boat. We strapped up our boat, The Soggy Sandwich, nice and tight and slowly pulled out of the driveway. We were going to spend the day fishing in the ocean, Pacific to be exact. This was going to be my first time to ride the ocean waves. We have a six seater cherry red speed boat with a fishing area. It goes eighty-five m.p.h. at top speed. My dad and I let it down into the clear blue ocean water and we were ready to go.

When we got in deeper water we changed the speed to forty. All of the sudden a blue location buoy jumped right out in front of us and, SMACK!

We flew into the air doing spirals like a football. We landed with a smack. The boat was horribly damaged and my dad was nowhere to be found! I was scared to death!

"Daaaaaaaaaaad" I screamed at the top of my lungs. I passed out on what was left of the boat.

"Wh-where am I," I silently whispered half asleep. "Where's my daddy?"

"He's fine. Just in the other room," said a nurse at Palm Bay Hospital. I had broken three bones and had twenty three stitches but my dad was just fine.

A lesson well learned: always watch the water in case anything jumps in front of you! You would not want to experience it.

Score for Writing Sample #4:   My Trip to the Ocean   (narrative)

Category	Questions	Answers	Points
FORMAT	Does this piece have a beginning that is to the point, introducing us to the topic?	yes	1
	Does this piece have a middle that tells a story or explains details and reasons?	yes	1
	Does this piece have an ending?	yes	1
CONTENT	Does the middle tell a complete story or explain the topic fully with details the reader can visualize?	yes	1
CREATIVITY	Are there **at least** four or five successful CREATIVITY SKILLS I can point to that helped make the writing mature and entertaining for the reader?	yes	1
MODEL	Is this paper OUTSTANDING?	no	-
CONVENTIONS	Did the writer have readable handwriting, capital letters, periods, grammar, and correct spelling MOST of the time?	yes	-

5

SCORE _5_

Strengths:

This writer kept me on the edge of my seat. He told a riveting story, and he told it well. He has delicious details. I could picture so many things he was writing about. And his dialogue was very authentic. Great use of onomatopoeia.

Weaknesses:

I so wanted to give this paper a six!!! The reason I had to hold the score back to a five is that I felt the writer didn't give nearly as many details about his rescue, time at the hospital, and his reunion with his dad as he told about the beginning of the story. We wanted to hear more!

Scorer's Comments:

Man, it's kids who write like this that make me love being a writing teacher. And guess what! I know a secret. This story didn't really happen. This 4th grade boy made it up! Talk about a great imagination!

Scoring Writing Sample #5

Your writing is getting better and better. One good way to improve your own writing is to read something terrific written by another kid. Here's a narrative piece that'll knock your socks off! It was written by a fourth grade girl who used lots of vivid details so you can picture just how horrible this experience was for her. Enjoy!

Narrative Prompt: Accidents happen! Think of a time you had an accident. Now write the story of your accident.

Beautiful Curls

Alas! My curls! They're gone forever! I'm sobbing just thinking about it.
Why am I mourning over curls do you ask? I'll explain. It was cool outside, and I was playing in our spacios backyard with Jason, my brother. We were playing hide and seek, and Jason was the seeker. I decided to go hide in the green bushes behind our splintered fence in the backyard. So I snuck behind the prickly bushes as sly as a fox and settled down to wait. Then Jason finally entered the backyard. After counting to 30, I had the sensation that I was slowly sinking. I glanced down. My shoulder length, brown-blond curls shined in the sunlight. As I looked down, my knees were just above a brown oozy mixture that resembled mud. Then it dawned on me. (pause 5 seconds right here) I was knee-deep in quicksand!

I didn't care if I won hide and seek. All that I cared about was that somebody found me in less than a milisecond. I started screaming at the top of lungs, "Jason, Jason!" with terror ringing in my voice. Jason came fast, even faster than a wild cheetah on the run. When he saw me with my curls all tangled in the bushes and waist high in quicksand he tried to hide his fear, but I saw it. Then he came back to his senses. He tried to pull me out but failed. You could see he was thinking. Only for a moment. As he was about to turn in the direction of the house he said, "Jessie, stop, breathe slowly, and I'll be back with mom in a flash." Jason ran like a bullet to mom. When mom saw Jason in his state of panic, she immediately knew something was wrong. Jason didn't even pause to explain. He grabbed mom's arm and practically dragged her in the backyard. She paused, wondering if I was stuck in the wooden fort. Mom looked hurriedly in the right and left corner of the wooden structure. I wasn't there. Then she started going crazy. By then I was chest high in the quicksand. Just when I thought they would never come they were pulling me out with mighty tugs. It was a miracle! I had been saved! My curls however, were not so lucky. The bushy leaves were actually sandspurs, and even after two baths, the burrs still wouldn't come out so my bouncy curls were snipped off with the dreaded scissors. From my past experience, I have learned that you should always, <u>always</u> look before you step.

Score for Writing Sample #5: Beautiful Curls (narrative)

Category	Questions	Answers	Points
FORMAT	Does this piece have a beginning that is to the point, introducing us to the topic?	yes	1
	Does this piece have a middle that tells a story or explains details and reasons?	yes	1
	Does this piece have an ending?	yes	1
CONTENT	Does the middle tell a complete story or explain the topic fully with details the reader can visualize?	yes	1
CREATIVITY	Are there **at least** four or five successful CREATIVITY SKILLS I can point to that helped make the writing mature and entertaining for the reader?	yes	1
MODEL	Is this paper OUTSTANDING?	yes	1
CONVENTIONS	Did the writer have readable handwriting, capital letters, periods, grammar, and correct spelling MOST of the time?	yes	-

6

SCORE __6__

Strengths:

Wow! I felt like I was the girl in the story, being sucked down in the deadly quicksand. This author painted the picture of her heart-stopping accident with vivid details! It sounded to me like the writer took her time, relived the accident in her imagination, and used language that was sizzling and specific. Anyone can see why this paper earned a 6.0!

Weaknesses:

It's hard to find any faults with this excellent story. Perhaps if the author indented more often the text might be easier to read.

Scorer's Comments:

Learn from an expert. This kid has got it going on when it comes to telling a great story! She gets right into the action. She included lots of creativity skills to add imagination and "snap," and she remembered to tell us the lesson she learned at the very end. As I said before, WOW!

Blank Score Sheet for young Writers

Category	Questions	Answers	Points
FORMAT	Does this piece have a beginning that is to the point, introducing us to the topic?	____	____
	Does this piece have a middle that tells a story or explains details and reasons?	____	____
	Does this piece have an ending?	____	____
CONTENT	Does the middle tell a complete story or explain the topic fully with details the reader can visualize?	____	____
CREATIVITY	Are there **at least** four or five successful CREATIVITY SKILLS I can point to that helped make the writing mature and entertaining for the reader?	____	____
MODEL	Is this paper OUTSTANDING?	____	____
CONVENTIONS	Did the writer have readable handwriting, capital letters, periods, grammar, and correct spelling MOST of the time?	____	____

SCORE ____

Strengths:

Weaknesses:

Scorer's Comments:

How to Budget your 45 Minutes

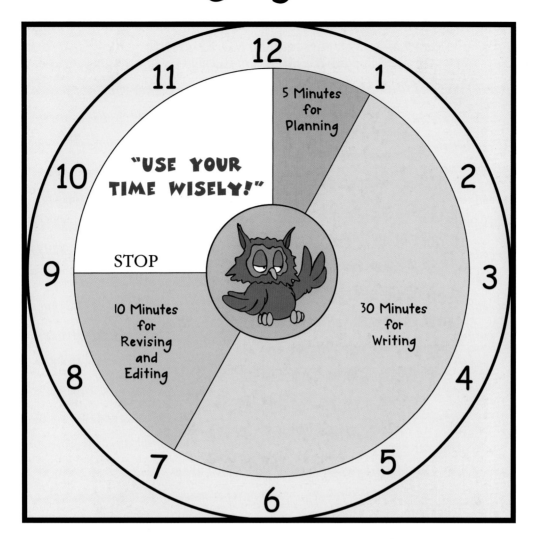

On the day of Florida Writes you will be allowed to write and work on your writing for 45 minutes. Now, what is the best way to make use of those minutes?

As you can see, the clock above is divided into sections. When you first read the prompt you will be given to write on, it will be tempting to get started on the writing part right away. STOP! Can you imagine an airplane pilot jumping in the cockpit and taking off as soon as he sits down? No way! He's got to stop and think about where he's headed, what the weather is like, and how much fuel he has. It takes preparation to fly a plane!

Before you write, take five minutes to think about the prompt and **plan** your strategy. Draw a quick storyboard or list the major points you want to remember when you write.

Next, **begin writing**. Use the next 25 minutes to **write** with pizzazz, impressing your reader with vivid descriptions, exciting actions, major points, and terrific examples.

Use the last ten minutes to *reread your paper*. Now is the time for you to **revise** and **edit**. Some kids don't want to do this, but be smart and do it anyway. **Look for ways to improve**. Cross out boring words, and change them to sizzling words. Add more information. Make sure you've used punctuation so your reader won't have trouble reading your paper.

6.0 Narrative Writing Sample

This narrative piece was written by a Florida girl in the 4th grade. I've labeled most of the writer's tricks that make it an outstanding 6.0. Read it for enjoyment, but also, pay attention to the skills the writer used to add beauty and enjoyment to her writing.

Narrative Prompt: Tell the story of something exciting that happened to you.

transitional phrase · transitional phrase

One sizzling summer day I was building a barn for my model horses. Just as I was

sizzle word · strong verb · strong verb

finishing up the stall door an irridescent glow illuminated the barn. Buried under the straw

onomatopoeia · creativity

was a golden horse shoe, but more than that. WOOSH! All was black...follow my hoofprints

beginning

while I tell you about when I had a great time making something.

transitional phrase

In the swish of a horse's tail, I was standing in front of a sign that read:

creativity · descriptive writing

"Horsetopia." In a valley below me I saw horses---thousands of horses in every color

descriptive writing · strong verb · descriptive writing

imaginable There were red duns grazing peacefully with their foals, rose grays and browns

descriptive writing · descriptive writing

drinking from a rushing waterfall, and a piebald dozing in the shade of a willow tree. Being

strong verb · descriptive writing

s-o-o-o mesmerized I didn't notice the shadowy figures of horses standing behind me. I

strong verb · strong verb · strong verb · transitional phrase

jumped up and whirled around to find two Arabians hovering over me. The first was a bay,

descriptive writing · descriptive writing · descriptive writing · transitional phrase

not a dark bay, but a clear bay whose coat was touched with gold. The second was

descriptive writing · descriptive writing · dialogue

different, a glowing red chestnut that made me think of fire. "I'm Flame and this is

strong verb

Sunshine," neighed the stallion.

dialogue · strong verb · descriptive writing

"Wh-w-WoW!" I stuttered. Would I ever ride this magical creature?

creativity · dialogue

In a hoofbeat, Flame asked, "Would you like a ride?"

...Narrative Writing Sample

dialogue   *strong verb*   *descriptive writing*   *descriptive writing*

"Sure!" As I mounted the mighty animal I looked beyond a moss covered stone wall

sizzle word   *descriptive writing*   *descriptive writing*

and saw a field of fluorescent flowers, some mares sipping water from a crystal clear

descriptive writing   *strong verb*   *strong verb*   *descriptive writing*

lake, and frisky foals frolicing in an orchard. We trotted down a rocky hillside overflowing

descriptive writing

with wild flowers.

strong verb   *strong verb*   *strong verb*   *simile*

Flame leaped over a log and cantered while Sunshine trotted behind, proud as a

descriptive writing   *simile*   *descriptive writing*

peacock. I looked down and saw Flame's sweat covered coat shining like a star twinkling in

descriptive writing   *dialogue*   *strong verb*   *voice*

the midnight sky. "You should race in the Horsetopia Handicap" nickered Sunshine. Will we

win the race?

creative transitional phrase

In the crack of a whip, Flame and I were being led into the starting gate. Then a

descriptive writing   *descriptive writing*   *metaphor*

stallion rose high, high into the air, teeth bared, hooves flailing. He was a giant of a

descriptive writing   *descriptive writing*

horse, glistening black--too big to be pure Arabian. He shook his head furiously, his black

simile   *dialogue*

mane flowing like a windswept flame. "And they're off!" yelled the emcee. "Thunder Gulch

voice

is in the lead with Whirlaway and Flame following behind. Wait! Flame is one-two-THREE

transitional phrase   *onomatopoeia*   *voice*

lengths ahead! He has won the race!" All of a sudden BANG! Everything went black...

creative transitional phrase

In a magical minute, I was staring into the barn wondering. What happened was

conclusion   *onomatopoeia*

extraordinary, for an ordinary day. I started to walk away when--THUD! I tripped over a

descriptive writing   *voice*

golden horseshoe. All I did was smile. C'est La Vie! (That's Life)

6.0 Expository Writing Sample

Enjoy reading this expository piece, a 6.0, that describes a place you may never get to visit. Then read it again, and see if you can spot all of the writer's tricks and skills. Give yourself five points for every skill you find. Use these skills in your own writing.

Expository Prompt: Write about a place or location that impresses you.

Under the Green Umbrella

Can you imagine something so breathtaking, something so awesome, that it's next to impossible to describe? That's what I experience when I walk through the tropical rainforests of Panama, Nature's wonderland, where I was born.

To begin with, being in the rainforest is like being under a giant green umbrella. The canopy of the trees that grows high over the understory is an ever-changing kaleidoscope of greens: olive, lime, chartreuse, forest, and many shades in between. Very little light filters down through the leafy branches, and the rainforest floor remains shady and humid, even on the hottest of days. I enjoy walking barefoot so I can feel the earth and shuffle through the fallen leaves.

No trip through the rainforests of Panama would be complete without the familiar sights and sounds of the animals that make the jungle their home. Slow-moving, scraggly-furred sloths lie sleeping in the high branches of a eucalyptus tree. A harpy eagle swoops in screeching, with his talons poised to pluck one of the sloths from his napping place. Howler monkeys swing from tree to tree, leaping and hooting as they hunt for

ripened fruit. Colorful toucans clack their long, curved beaks.
CLAT! CLAT! They sit on swaying branches, looking just like
they stepped off the front of a box of Froot Loops. Flocks
of green parrots and scarlet macaws fly overhead, brilliantly plumed,
screaming their distinctively loud calls.

All of these things you can see up overhead, but the rainforest is
home to a host of other animals and insects you can see at close range.
Green tree snakes, s-shaped, wrap themselves around thin tree trunks,
waiting for unsuspecting frogs. Rhinoceros beetles lumber across the humid
path, clumsy and comical. Their sturdy size and frontal rhino horn make
them look much like their giant African namesakes. Armies of leaf-cutter
ants carry leaf "umbrellas" over their heads. They march to and fro in ant
lines that can stretch for over a mile.

The sounds of the rainforest are melodic. A waterfall whispers in the
background. Rain drops drip from the lacy leaves of a mimosa tree. Ripe
fruit falls to the ground.

The smells of the rainforest are strange: the humid earth, the
rotting leaves, overripe fruit, and the musky smell of a coati mundi.

Even though I am grown now and no longer live there, the rainforest
calls to me still, amazing, breathtaking, and stunningly beautiful.

It is indeed Nature's wonderland.

Alligator Score Chart

This score chart is fun to make and a blast to use. It gives you an idea of just what to look for when you're writing so you can make the highest score. You will need your teacher to help you with the directions.

Instructions for Making a Score Chart

For this project you'll need:

scissors   glue
tape   colored paper

1. Copy the four pieces of the score chart on stiff, colored paper. You can use any different colors of paper you like but make sure it's stiff.

2. You'll need one **extra** piece of colored, stiff paper as a backpiece.

3. Cut out pieces #1, #2, #3, and #4.

4. Glue piece #1 to the backpiece, all the way to the right.

5. Make the slider, which is piece #3. Cut it out. Fold it in half. Fold it in half again. Fold it in half again. Now cut through the fold on cut #1 and cut #2. That's it!

6. Open the slider so that it is just folded in half two times. Push the center part down while holding the sides.

7. Cut out the arrow, and tape it to the right edge of the slider. Tape it on the back, and let it stick out to the right.

8. Fold the side flaps to the back on piece #2. Crease the folds.

9. Fit the slider over piece #2 so that the center part is to the back, and it will slide up and down. The arrow should point to the right.

10. Tape piece #2 across the top and bottom next to piece #3 that has already been glued down on the backpiece. The slider should move easily up and down

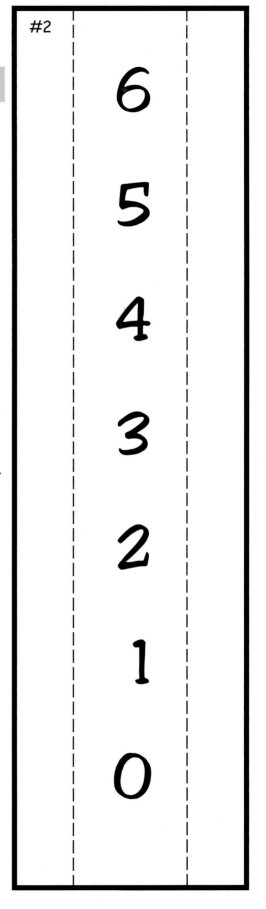

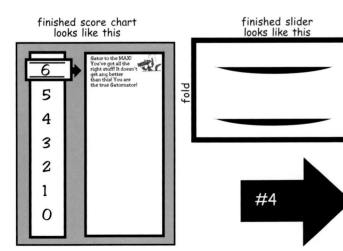

finished score chart
looks like this

finished slider
looks like this

Gator to the MAX!
You've got all the
right stuff! It doesn't
get any better
than this! You are
the true Gatornator!

#4

...ALLIGATOR SCORE CHART

#1

Gator to the MAX! You've got all the right stuff! It doesn't get any better than this! You are the true Gatornator!

 extraordinary details, many examples, organized, razzle dazzles the reader
BEGINNING, FAT MIDDLE, ENDING, VERY CREATIVE

Super Duper, Gator! You're on your way to the top. Next time, put the pedal to the metal and bring it on home.

 super details, several examples, organized, has pizzazz
BEGINNING, FAT MIDDLE, ENDING, CREATIVITY

Woo hoo! We hear you loud and clear. Next time impress us with a little more sparkle. Strut your stuff. Go, Gator!

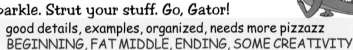

 good details, examples, organized, needs more pizzazz
BEGINNING, FAT MIDDLE, ENDING, SOME CREATIVITY

Looking better! We know what you're trying to say. Next time, put some more meat on the bones.

 adequate but lacks completeness and sparkle, some details
BEGINNING, MIDDLE, ENDING

You're trying! Now let's get organized. Next time, let's see a few more juicy details and examples. You can do it!

 inadequate, illogical, frequent errors, some details
BEGINNING and SKINNY MIDDLE, MAYBE an ENDING

You're still in the doghouse, Gator! You tried a little bit, but you need more "snap" to your bite!

 very little written, no organization, few details, errors
SHORT BEGINNING, SHORT MIDDLE

See you later, Gator! There's nothing here to score, dude, or you got totally off topic. You can do better, for sure.

 nothing written on topic, unscorable
NO BEGINNING, MIDDLE, or ENDING

Make your Own Score Tower

Wait till you see how awesome this score tower looks when you get it put together. It gives you an idea of just what to include in your writing so you can make the highest score. You will need your teacher to help you with the directions.

Instructions for Making a Score Tower

For this project you'll need:

scissors	animal cutouts
glue stick or tape	stiff paper

1. Copy the animal cutouts below onto stiff paper.

2. Cut out the animal cutouts. Fold the bottom tab back on the fold line. Set aside.

3. Copy page 185 onto a whole sheet of stiff paper.

4. Fold on the fold line in the middle of the sheet. Fold it both ways, inside and out.

5. Your sheet should now be folded in half so you can read the words.

6. Using your scissors, cut along the dark lines up to the top fold line. This makes three "bars."

7. Fold the "bars" up along the fold lines at the top. Crease this top fold line.

8. Now open the entire sheet half way and "pop up" the bars. Cool, huh?

9. Glue or tape (or both) the animal cutout tabs to the TOP of each "pop up" bar.

10. Use the tower to remind you what you need to score high!

4

fold

glue

5

fold

glue

6

fold

glue

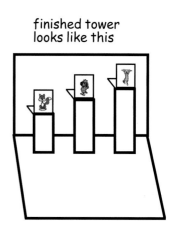

finished tower looks like this

Score Tower

cut

cut

glue fox tab

fold

4

Beginning

Middle

Ending

Content

Completeness

top fold

cut

cut

glue toucan tab

fold

5

Beginning

Middle

Ending

Details

Super
Content

Creativity

Sizzling
Vocabulary

top fold

cut

cut

glue tiger tab

fold

6

Beginning

Middle

Ending

Details

Super
Content

Creativity

Sizzling
Vocabulary

Imagination

Outstanding!

fold

CHECK OUT WHAT YOU NEED TO GET ONE OF THESE SCORES!

Writing Medallions

FOCUS ON THE PROMPT

FLORIDA WRITES SCORING RUBRIC

6 = OUTSTANDING

5 = VERY GOOD

4 = GOOD

3 = OKAY

2 = NOT TOO GOOD

1 = POOR

0 = DISASTER

NEVER BE AFRAID TO ASK FOR HELP!

DO NOT DISTURB: WRITER AT WORK!

DON'T "BEE" LAZY!

If you can spell something CORRECTLY, that's great. If there's a big, juicy word you want to use and you can't think of how to spell it, listen to the way it SOUNDS. Use letters that sound like the word so your readers can figure out what you mean.

Write your paper without worrying too much about spelling. The most important thing is for you to get your thoughts down. When you finish, then go back and check to see if you have spelled things correctly.

PUT YOUR BEST FOOT FORWARD!

It is better to GUESS at the spelling of a creative, sizzling word than to use a simple, boring word that you are sure you can spell.
Writing Superstars
TAKE RISKS!

COME OUT OF YOUR SHELL... WRITE WITH DESCRIPTION!

1. Be prepared. Show up with your pencil, paper, and supplies.

2. Do your best. Never give less than your best writing effort.

3. Have a good attitude. Be a good example to other writers.

4. Stay on task. It's simple! During writing time, focus on learning all you can learn every single day.

5. Get in shape. You are here to learn new skills. Learn them well.

6. Help your buddies.

7. Be creative. Use your imagination at all times.

8. Receive suggestions and criticism with courtesy.

9. Teach the skills you learn to someone else.

10. Remember: You are now preparing for your own TERRIFIC FUTURE!

Songs for Genius Writers

We're Going to Write Like Maniacs Tonight!
Sung to the tune of Rock Around the Clock

One o'clock, two o'clock, three o'clock WRITE (jump on Write)
Four o'clock, five o'clock, six o'clock WRITE (jump on Write)
Seven o'clock, eight o'clock, nine o'clock WRITE (jump on Write)
We're going to write around the clock tonight

When the clock strikes eight, don't be late
We're going to start to concentrate
We're going to write around the clock tonight
Going to write, write, write till broad daylight
Going to write, going to write like maniacs tonight

When the clock strikes ten, grab your pen
We're going to write a rough draft and then
We're going to check it twice, please be nice
Going to write, write, write some sugar and spice
Going to write, going to write like maniacs tonight

When the clock strikes one, and we're done
We're going to have a barrel of fun
We're going to use our skill, what a thrill
Going to write, write, write you know the drill
Going to write, going to write like maniacs tonight

A Kid Named Ted
Sung to the tune of The Beverly Hillbillies

Come and listen to my story 'bout a kid named Ted
Writing skills were a-buzzin' in his head
Beginning, middle, ending and a little bit more,
When the scores came back our Ted got a four
        (Four point oh, that is, absolutely admirable)

Well Ted's best bud was a girl named Mary
She wrote so well it was gettin' kind of scary
Her papers were jammin' with details and jive
When the scores came back she was lookin' at a five
        (Five point oh, unbelievably fanciful)

Now Ted and Mary had a pal named Joe,
The best dang writer any kid could ever know
He wrote so much he was never in a fix
When the scores came back they cried, "It's a six!"
        (Six point oh, that is, positively preposterous...top dawg!)

Adding the Writing Skills that you Have Learned
Sung to the tune of My Favorite Things

VERSE ONE

Capital letters and end punctuation
Will help your reader avoid aggravation
Sizzling verbs, metaphors, similes,
Help you score four-or-more with perfect ease

Commas in a series and sentence variety
Win you the prize in a writing society
Organization can help you succeed
Onomatopoeia is great, yes, indeed

VERSE TWO

Try to avoid using tacky expressions
Specific emotion words make good impressions
Using a "grabber" is simply superb
Adjectives dazzle and so do adverbs

If your prompt is one that's expository
Supporting with details will add extra glory
Narrative writing should sparkle and gleam
Causing your reader to shout, "It's supreme!"

CHORUS

When you're writing
    it's inviting
Just to write and stop
But adding the writing skills
    that you have learned
Will help you score at the top

Florida Writes!
Sung to the tune of The Addams' Family

Florida Writes! (snap, snap)
Florida Writes! (clap, clap)
Florida Writes!
Florida Writes!
Florida Writes! (stomp, stomp)
It comes in February
4th graders must be wary
It really isn't scary
Just do your very best
You'll use imagination
And super concentration
Your powers of creation
Will help you do your best

It's not a competition
It's just an exhibition
So lose your inhibitions
And do your very best
You want to get a score
Of four and maybe more
A six you would adore
So do your very best
Florida Writes! (snap, snap)
Florida Writes! (clap, clap)
Florida Writes!
Florida Writes!
Florida Writes! (stomp, stomp)

...Songs for Genius Writers

All For Florida Writes!
Sung to the tune of Gilligan's Island

Just sit right back and you'll hear a tale
A tale of a 4th grade class
Whose lofty goal for Florida Writes
   Was every kid would pass (was every kid would pass)
   The kids were writing superstars
   The teacher, tried and true
   But they faced the test in seven months
    A really tough thing to do (a really tough thing to do)
   They learned to write with content
   And creativity
   Their beginnings, middles, and endings
  Were the best that they could be (the best that they could be)
  They hoped for lots of fours and fives in the mix
With sizzling words and dialogue
Some might get a six (some might get a six)
These writers practiced every day with positive delight
On similes, and metaphors
Strong verbs and dialogue
Descriptive words, punctuation and takeaways
All for Florida Writes!

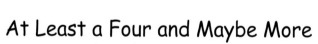

At Least a Four and Maybe More
Lyrics by Aaron Odom
Freestyle Rapped to a Beat Box

I'm Joe MC, that is my name
And rockin' it for you could be my game
Could be my game, so what do you like?
Cause Joe MC is on the mike

Now writing skills I'm gonna say
Are really what takes my breath away
My breath's away so don't look down
My paper's gonna be the best in town

The best in town, my name in lights
I'm a-gettin' ready for the Florida Writes
Now Florida Writes is what I been screamin'
A four or more is cool so ain't nobody dreamin'

Dreamin'...plannin', I'm checking it twice
Fittna' write a story that's as cold as ice
I said cold as ice, you know I'm Joe MC
No one's gonna take my score away from me

Away from me? Don't touch my score
I say at least a four and maybe more
At least a four and maybe more
At least a four and maybe more
At least a four it's in the mix
Who know's maybe I will get a five or six
Who know's maybe I will get a five or six

...Songs for Genius Writers

Bill Grogan's Goat

Sung to the tune of Bill Grogan's Goat
(music and words on p. 212)
Bill Grogan's Goat can also be read as a poem.

Bill Grogan's goat
He wrote so fine
Instead of "six"
He got a "nine"
Bill bragged and bragged
And flipped his lid
Because his goat
Was one smart "kid"
He took him to
The nearest school
And said, "This goat
Is not a fool!
Your kids should see
How well he writes
His dialogue
Is dynamite
He uses 'voice'
With perfect ease
Transition words?
For him a breeze!
His sizzling verbs
Are filled with bliss
Can 4th grade kids
Write verbs like this?"

The teacher said,
"With your permission
I'd like to stage
A competition
We will go by
A judges' vote
My 4th grade kids
Against your goat!"
Bill Grogan clapped,
The children danced
The genius goat
Got up and pranced
He strutted 'round
And puffed his chest
And said, "You'll see
That I write best!"
But as they started
With their caper
And kids took out
Their stacks of paper
The goat began
To chomp and munch
Until he'd eaten
Up the bunch

He said, "This paper
I adore!
Please tell me that
There's much, much more!"
He ate it all
Yes, every sheet
Then burped real loud
And gave a bleet
The children laughed
With such delight
And said, "Who cares
If goats can write?
Can you believe
This great surprise?
He's eaten all
Our school supplies!"
And so they never
Really knew
If goats can write
But, hey, it's true
Some goats can write
So very fine
Instead of "six"
They get a "nine"

The Boot Camp Song

Sung to the tune of Yankee Doodle Dandy

I'm a razzle dazzle writer
And I want to do my best
Our class is learning how to write, write, write
So we'll score high on the test (Florida Writes!)
We use our class's marching orders
They will help us all go far
We're the kids who write with content
We use punctuation
I am a Writing Superstar!

I'm a razzle dazzle writer
And I really must confess
Our class is hoping we will score, score, score
Four, Five, or Six with SUCCESS (Florida Writes!)
We know that we should stay on topic
And to edit when we're done
We're the kids who are creative
We support with details
Come join our 4th grade writing fun!

So you Think you Can Grab

A Three-Minute Play by Melissa Forney

Characters: Hostess Georgina   Judge Bad Boy Zee
Contestant Gill   Judge Ian Suave
Contestant Katy   Judge Liz Starlet
Contestant Seth   Audience

Setting: A popular reality television show

Georgina: Welcome to America's number one television program, "So You Think You Can Grab," the show where we're looking for the best grabbers in America! Ladies and Gentlemen, your judges: Bad Boy Zee, Ian Suave, and Liz Starlet!

Audience: (applause, cheers)

Georgina: Our first contestant is that wonder-of-wonders writer....Gill from Gillette!

Audience: (applause, cheers, etc.)

Georgina: Gill, what have you got for us tonight?

Gill: Georgina, I'm going to do what I do best, and that's grab the audience's attention. Here's my grabber: "Hello! My name is Gill! I'm going to tell you three main reasons why Florida is a great place to live."

Audience: (polite applause)

Georgina: Judges, let's hear your reactions. Ian?

Ian: I'm sorry, Gill. You've got a great personality, we've loved you all the way through auditions, but tonight you left me cold. (audience boos) That's my opinion! It's a no for me. Your grabber's just not good enough.

Georgina: Liz?

Liz: Gill, I've been a big fan of yours. But I'll have to agree with Ian tonight. It was just okay, not enough to get you into the finals. Sorry.

Georgina: Zee?

Zee: So here's what's up, Gill. You just weren't cool. You're never going to get someone's attention by starting out with "Hello, my name is Gill." But the worst part for me was saying "three main reasons." Put a chill on that. We *get it.* You don't have to *tell us* you're giving three reasons.

Georgina: Okay, Gill. Sorry, but you just didn't cut it with the judges tonight. Next up is Katy-Katy-Bo-datey, that sizzling writer from Kissimmee. Katy, the spotlight is on YOU! Do your stuff and show us a great grabber.

Katy: Hello, America! I've been working on my grabber all week. Okay, here goes: "Can you imagine what it's like to be trapped in a dark house during a hurricane when an oak tree crashes down on top of you?"

Audience: (applause)

..."Grab"

Georgina:	I loved it! Let's see what our judges think. Ian?
Ian:	Katy, I worried about you at this stage of the competition. (excited) But you nailed it! You were outstanding! That's the way to write a grabber! (audience applauds and cheers)
Georgina:	Liz?
Liz:	(sad voice) Katy, some grabbers just don't get it for me. (big pause) But yours was......(screams) WONDERFUL!!!! (audience applauds and cheers)
Georgina:	That's two out of three. Let's see what Zee has to say.
Zee:	You caused us to use our imaginations, you kept us on the edge of our seats, and as far as I'm concerned, Katy, that's the BEST grabber I've heard this season! (audience goes wild)
Georgina:	Well, save some of that excitement for our last contestant, that superlative superstar from Sarasota, Seth! (clapping) Seth, we've heard from Gill, we've heard from Katy. Now it's your turn to show us your stuff!
Seth:	Well, first I'd like to say a big hello to my parents. They're here in the audience. Mom, Dad, thanks for always believing in me. I wouldn't be able to grab an audience without your examples over the years.
Georgina:	How wonderful that your mum and dad are here, Seth. Now make them proud! Give us your best grabber.
Seth:	Mom, Dad, this one's for you. "What first started out as an ordinary Friday night turned into a nightmare, a nightmare that will haunt me for as long as I live." (audience goes crazy)
Georgina:	Well done! And as always, let's turn to our judges. Ian?
Ian:	Seth, we've had our eye on you from the beginning. You never disappoint. It's writers like you who remind us how smart kids are. I think you've got what it takes to actually win this competition. (thunderous applause)
Georgina:	Liz?
Liz:	There's only one way to describe that grabber: Aaaaaah! (screams) (cheering and clapping from the audience)
Georgina:	Zee?
Zee:	I've heard a lot of grabbers, but that one is the bomb! I think you're the man! (audience cheers, etc.) Definitely the man!
Georgina:	Well, our judges are impressed, but the final decision is up to YOU, America. Vote for the person you think has the best grabber: Gill, Katy, or Seth. The number is on your screen. Tune in tomorrow night to see who is going home and who will go on to the finals on...So You Think You Can Grab!
Audience:	(cheering, whistles, clapping, etc.)

Writing Precinct

A Five-Minute Play by Melissa Forney

Characters: Announcer   Dispatcher   Vonya
                  Officer Jenko   Officer Romano   Mrs. Hudson

Setting: The New York City patrol car of officers Jenko and Romano

SCENE ONE

Announcer:	Writing Precinct is a group of dedicated professionals committed to the well being of writing projects, protecting the innocent, and keeping standards high. We join Officers Pat Jenko and J.T. Romano on an ordinary day as they cruise the streets of The Big Apple.
Dispatcher:	T-G-9 Papa Echo. Officers needed. Please respond.
Officer Jenko:	Unit Nine responding. Go ahead.
Dispatcher:	Officers needed at Bonner Elementary. What's your 20?
Officer Jenko:	We're at 5th and Main. What's the problem?
Dispatcher:	We've received an anonymous call about some neglected writing. Possible abuse. Officers needed on the scene immediately.
Officer Jenko:	We're on it. I'll call if we need backup.
Dispatcher:	Officer? The caller mentioned something about 4th grade. Take every precaution.
Officer Jenko:	Roger that. Over.
Officer Romano:	Time to rock and roll?
Officer Jenko:	Bonner Elementary. Writing neglect.
Officer Romano:	Third time this week. Remember that personal narrative?
Officer Jenko:	The kid who wrote one rough draft and told his teacher he was done?
Officer Romano:	That's the one. No imagination. No creativity.
Officer Jenko:	U-u-u-GLY! (he shudders) I still have nightmares.
Officer Romano:	We've got to get that kind of writing off the streets.
Officer Jenko:	I don't get it. Don't these kids know that being able to write well is going to help them get a good job one day?
Officer Romano:	Remember Charlie, from over in vice? His kid Donnie is all grown up now. Owns his own business. Makes good money. What a writer he was.

SCENE TWO   **...Writing Precinct**

Announcer:	The officers enter the halls of Bonner Elementary.
Officer Romano:	Let's split up. This writing could be anywhere.
Officer Jenko:	Dispatch said it was 4th grade.
Officer Romano:	Do we need to call for backup? Those can be kind of rough.
Officer Jenko:	Let's investigate, first.
Officer Romano:	Here's the hall bulletin board...(pause) No problem here.
Officer Jenko:	I just checked Mrs. Dawson's 4th grade classroom...Nothing out of the ordinary there...
Officer Romano:	I'll try the writers' notebooks in Mrs. Hudson's room.
Officer Jenko:	I'll search the homework bin in Mr. Scott's room.
	(PAUSE)
Officer Romano:	(shouting) Pat? PAT? (pause) (screams) GET IN HERE!
Officer Jenko:	(shouts) J.T.! What is it?
Officer Romano:	(horrified) For the love of Pete! Would you look at this.
Officer Jenko:	(frantic) Where? What?
Officer Romano:	Right here. See? It's neglect, all right. No CONCLUSION.
Officer Jenko:	Are you sure? I think I see something. Shine the light on the ending.
Officer Romano:	Read it and weep. No CONCLUSION.
Officer Jenko:	"I hope you liked my story. Bye. Gotta go now. The End."
Officer Romano:	What did I tell you? DISGUSTING.
Officer Jenko:	You're right, Partner. We might allow this in a second grade story, but 4th grade? No way! Any 4th grade kid should know better.
Officer Romano:	The author leaves me no choice. I'm taking this paper into custody.
Officer Jenko:	Tomorrow we'll find the student who wrote this paper.
Officer Romano:	You know this is going to be hard on Mrs. Hudson.
Officer Jenko:	She teaches her heart out. Yeah, she's going to take it pretty hard. My sister's kids had Mrs. Hudson, and she was terrific. You should see those kids write. Fantastic.

SCENE THREE   **...Writing Precinct**

Announcer:	The next day Officer Jenko and his partner, Officer Romano, enter the room of Emaline Hudson, 4th grade teacher at Bonner Elementary.
Officer Jenko:	Pardon me, ma'am. Do you have any idea who wrote this paper?
Mrs. Hudson:	Why yes, that's my student, Vonya Lark.
Officer Jenko:	May I speak with Miss Lark?
Mrs. Hudson:	Here's Vonya now, but what's this about, Officer?
Officer Jenko:	Mrs. Hudson, Miss Lark, I'm Officer Pat Jenko and this is Officer J.T. Romano from the Writing Precinct. Do you recognize this paper?
Vonya:	I think so. That looks like the one I wrote for you, Mrs. Hudson.
Mrs. Hudson:	It sure does, Vonya. I saw you working on that paper just yesterday.
Officer Romano:	Uh, Miss Lark, I'm afraid we're going to have to take this paper into custody. There's a severe lack of conclusion.
Mrs. Hudson:	No conclusion? Vonya, I've reminded you about that time after time.
Vonya:	(whiny) I couldn't think of anything, Mrs. Hudson. Besides, I was tired of writing and wanted to play with the tangrams. (desperate) Can't I have another chance, officer? Please? PLEASE?
Officer Romano:	Maybe when you've learned how to write a proper conclusion, Miss Lark, but we're taking this paper into custody.
Officer Jenko:	A conclusion tells the reader the most important thing you want him to know. You might try remembering that next time, Miss Lark.
Mrs. Hudson:	How many times have we been over this, Vonya?
Vonya:	Can't I keep my writing? (cries loudly) I didn't think it mattered!
Officer Jenko:	Sorry, kid. This paper will be given critical care and then adopted out to some other student who knows how to take care of her writing.
Vonya:	But I'll try harder next time! (sobs) I want my paper back!!!
Mrs. Hudson:	I'll have to agree with the officers, Vonya. You've been warned.
Officer Romano:	It's a hard lesson to learn. Tough break, Kid.
Announcer:	Vonya's paper was indeed taken into custody where it was given immediate first aid by another 4th grade writer. In a few days the paper had gained details, description, and a proper conclusion. The paper now has a good home and resides somewhere in the Miami area. Join us again next week for another exciting Writing Precinct rescue.

Survivor: Expository Island

A Five-Minute Play by Melissa Forney

Characters: Jeff Probe a Lot   Dirk Muscularis
                    Rodney Attorney   Tammy Teacher
                    Bubba Goodoldboy   Harriet Housewife

Setting: A tropical island somewhere in the South Pacific

Jeff Probe A Lot: Sixteen castaways thrown together on a tropical island for 39 days with a single goal: to win a million dollars. Two tribes of eight members compete in reward challenges and immunity challenges to determine which group will have to face Tribal Council. In tonight's episode, the losers, the Chaka-Khans, must vote off one team member. (to team) Survivors, light your torches and take a seat. Frankly, I'm surprised you're here. Yesterday you won the reward challenge. Today you were defeated by the Doo-Wah-Diddies and must now vote off one of your own members. But first, let's find out your reactions and how things are going. Dirk, how do you feel about today's defeat?

Dirk Muscularis: Uh, Jeff, that hurt. I'll have to admit it. I hate to lose.

Jeff Probe A Lot: Do you feel like any one particular member of the Chaka-Khans caused your defeat?

Dirk Muscularis: No one likes to point fingers, but...well...take Rodney, for instance. I just don't think he can go the distance. In today's challenge you asked for specific details and reasons about yesterday's reward challenge, and Rodney used phrases like, "We had a good time," and, "It was awesome." That's sure not giving 100%.

Jeff Probe A Lot: Rodney, how do you respond to that?

Rodney Attorney: Well, Jeff, I don't know how to respond. I thought I was giving *120%!*

Tammy Teacher: 120%? No way. I won't let you weasel out of this one, Rodney. You should have given specific examples like, "The swimming relay was challenging because we had to swim a quarter of a mile in tropical waters. Each one of us felt extremely proud when we won the reward."

Rodney Attorney: Well, what about Bubba? His reasons were pitiful.

Jeff Probe A Lot: A pretty strong accusation. Bubba, would you care to respond?

Bubba Goodoldboy: I'd say that city slicker's slinging some mud from his own garden. Those are fightin' words where I come from.

Rodney Attorney: Cut the cornpone, Bubba. Let's let the evidence speak for itself. You wrote, "I sure did love the reward prize." You call THAT a specific detail? What a hayseed!

Bubba Goodoldboy: (sarcastic) Well, Mr. Courtroom, if you'd bothered to read further you'd have seen that I AMPLIFIED my writing. I made a statement and then supported it with specific reasons and details.

Harriet Housewife: I'll have to agree. If you'd read further, Rodney, you would have seen that Bubba followed up, "I sure did love the reward prize," with, "Those cheeseburgers and fries were pure heaven," and "I can still taste that red, ripe tomato and those slices of dill pickles. We're talking scrumptious!"

Dirk Muscularis: Busted, Rodney! That writing is specific, descriptive, and if I'm not mistaken, "pure heaven" is a metaphor. Way to go, Bubba!

Tammy Teacher: Not to mention the word "scrumptious." His sizzling vocabulary is hot, hot, hot! Bubba, I think your attention to details actually won that reward challenge for us yesterday.

Bubba Goodoldboy: I was so hungry I could have eaten a buttered skunk!

Jeff Probe A Lot: You'll get the chance to do just that on next week's show, Bubba.

Harriett Housewife: Any reader could *picture* what Bubba was describing.

Dirk Muscularis: Wish I could taste it!

Tammy Teacher: Bubba's details ARE very specific. His writing is interesting and mature. A good example for us all.

Bubba Goodoldboy: Read 'em and weep, Rodney.

Jeff Probe A Lot: I think your tribe mates are trying to tell you that you owe Bubba an apology, Rodney.

Rodney Attorney: Me? Apologize to that grizzled old hayseed? Fat chance.

Bubba Goodoldboy: I might be a hayseed, but I'm going to be a hayseed wearing an Armani suit when I win that million dollars.

Rodney Attorney: Hey, if they want to vote against me, bring it on. But I'd like for Chaka-Khan to know that I am capable of writing specific reasons and details when I want to. It's just that I was feeling kind of...lazy. It takes energy to think of specific details.

Harriet Housewife: Hold the phone. Are you saying that you caused us to lose the immunity challenge because you were lazy?

Rodney Attorney: You guys have a conspiracy against me. I smell an alliance.

Jeff Probe A Lot: It's time to vote. Tammy, you're up first.

Tammy Teacher: (in the voting booth) Sorry, Rodney. You're the king of narrative writing, but when it comes to expository writing you've got to support with specific reasons and details. Tonight my vote goes to you.

Jeff Probe A Lot: Dirk, you're next.

...Survivor: Expository Island

Dirk Muscularis: Every team has a weak link, Rodney, and you're it, my man. You could have led our team to victory, but you took the easy way out. Nothing personal. I've got to think of what's best for the team.

Jeff Probe A Lot: Harriet, head on over to the voting booth.

Harriet Housewife: Writing takes effort, Rodney. You should know that. How do you ever prepare your briefs for the courtroom? Lazy writing never pays off. That's why my vote's for you.

Jeff Probe A Lot: Bubba, your turn.

Bubba Goodoldboy: You might be Mr. Fancy Lawyer Courtroom-King, and I may be a tractor-driving sod buster, but guess who's still in the game.

Jeff Probe A Lot: Rodney, you're up.

Rodney Attorney: (in voting booth) Tammy, tonight my vote's for you. You've been getting on my case from the beginning, and I've had it up to here. Enough's enough. Time to go, Sweetheart. You're outta here!

Jeff Probe A Lot: I'll go tally the votes. (pause) The first vote is for Rodney....Rodney....Tammy...Rodney...and the fourth person voted out of Chaka-Khan is...Rodney. The tribe has spoken. Please extinguish your torch and leave immediately.

Rodney Attorney: (to his teammates) Sorry, guys. I let the team down. I just want you to know that I don't blame you for voting me out tonight. I should have done some prewriting about the reward prize. That was the most delicious meal I can remember, and writing about it should have been a piece of cake. I hope you'll get in touch when all of this is over. Being one of the contestants on Expository Island has been one of the best experiences of my life. You guys have been awesome. Take care, and see you back in L.A.

Jeff Probe A Lot: Join us next week for another exciting adventure on Survivor: Expository Island. Next week contestants will face the most difficult challenge yet: Amplifying their writing and staying on topic at the same time. Would you like to win a million dollars? CBS is in the process of taking applications for next season's show, the most grueling Survivor yet, Survivor: Florida Writes! Contestants will be given 25 students each to prepare for a state writing test in just five shorts months. Tune in to see which of the tribe members earns a million dollars and which ones need therapy for life. (Survivor Music)

American Narrative Idol

A Five-Minute Play by Melissa Forney

Characters: Randy Tackman   Paula Abschool   Simon Growl
Ryan Seebest   Stella Star
Crissie Country   Long-Haired Rocker Guy

Setting: The television set of America's #1 Writing Show

Ryan: Good evening. Welcome to American Narrative Idol! I'm your host, Ryan Seebest, and I'd like to introduce our fine judges. Put your hands together for Randy Tackman, Paula Abschool, and Simon Growl!

Audience: Yeah! (claps, cheers)

Randy: Hey, Simon. Why did the chicken cross the playground? To get to the other slide. Get it? The other **slide?**

Simon: (English accent) You're pathetic.

Paula: Randy, why did the ballerina wear a tu-tu?

Randy: I'll bite, Dawg. Why?

Paula: Because three-threes were too BIG, and one-ones were too small!

Randy: WOOF-WOOF-WOOF. Good one!

Simon: Please. I feel a bout of nausea coming on. Ryan, you'd better rescue us here.

Ryan: Welcome, judges! Let's get started, then. It's time now to meet our first contestant. She's no stranger. All the way from Ocala, Florida, here's the super starlet herself, Stella Star!

Stella: Hi, everybody!

Ryan: How's it going, Stella? Are you having fun here in Hollywood?

Stella: It's a dream come true, Ryan. I'm having a blast.

Ryan: What's the best part?

Stella: Getting to see Hollywood. Meeting the other contestants.

Ryan: Is the competition tough?

Stella: You bet. We all want to be the next American Narrative Idol.

Ryan: Well, tonight we're looking for good narrative beginnings. This week's theme is about walking home from school. Now is a good time to ask our judges exactly what they're looking for. Randy, what advice can you offer?

Randy: Ryan my man, the beginning of a story has got to capture my attention. If you reel me in with the first sentence or two, you're one of my "dawgs," for sure.

...American Narrative Idol

Ryan: Good answer. Paula, what's your take on things?

Paula: I'll echo what Randy said, Ryan. The beginning of a story has got to make me want to keep reading.

Ryan: Simon, any tips for a kid who wants to start a story?

Simon: I think, for me, at least....there has to be some...sizzle. Yes, I'll say sizzle. I'm sick of hearing the same old beginnings of stories. Give us a break!

Ryan: Okay, Stella, you're up. Studio Audience, let's make this place thunder for....Stella Star!

Audience: (wild applause)

Stella: Okay...here goes. "Once upon a time there was a real cute girl named Jennifer and her best friends were Amber, Tamara, Cassidy, Kim, and Allyson. They were walking home from school one afternoon and they passed a haunted house. They decided to go in."

Ryan: Thank you, Stella Star. Judges? What do you have to say?

Randy: Just keeping it real, Stella, I was bored to death. I mean, you're in the 4th grade and you should be beyond all of that "Once upon a time" stuff. And I'm sick of the word "cute." You can do better.

Ryan: Paula?

Paula: Stella, you're a sweetheart, but when you write a narrative, it's best to focus on one or two characters. Don't list the names of all of your friends.

Ryan: Thank you, Paula. Simon?

Simon: Really, Stella, it was dreadful. If this is the way you write, I think you'll be going home.

Audience: Boo!!!!! (stomps feet)

Simon: I'm not being cruel. You'll see that in the long-run—I'm right.

Ryan: Whoa, Stella. Some heavy-handed suggestions from our judges. Okay, studio audience, you can vote for Stella right after our show. And now, from sunny California, here's our next contestant.....Long-Haired Rocker Guy!

Audience: (huge applause) Woo hoo!!

Ryan: Guy, it's good to have you on our show.

Guy: It's been amazing. Awesome. Even incredible. I'm having a terrific time. Amazing. Radical.

Ryan: Now I see why you did so well on descriptive adjective night. Guy, go ahead.

...American Narrative Idol

Guy: This is a new beginning I've been working on. Here goes. "Tommy Joe bounced as he walked home. School was over for the summer. No more homework. No more teachers. He whistled as he walked, but all of a sudden he stopped bouncing and walking. He stopped whistling, too. Instead, he leaned forward and squinted at what he saw sitting under the bush that grew near the sidewalk. His mouth opened in surprise. "Look at this," he said to himself. "I've never seen this before, and I've passed by this bush a thousand times!"

Audience: Wow! Yay! (claps and cheers)

Ryan: Thank you, Long-Haired Rocker Guy! Judges, let's hear your feedback.

Randy: Guy, I've got to hand it to you. That beginning kept me on the edge of my seat. I don't know what Tommy Joe *saw*, but I'm ready to keep reading to find out.

Ryan: Paula?

Paula: First of all, Guy, you come out on stage and are so at ease, you look great, you have such heart, but best of all, you take risks. I like that. Your beginning has a lot of description and mystery. Outstanding.

Ryan: Simon?

Simon: Guy, I'm finally listening to something I can connect with and visualize. When you said Tommy Joe was bouncing along, I actually saw that in my mind. When you said he was whistling, I could hear a happy, fun-loving kid who was free from all the worries of school. Guy, I think you've shown that kids can write great beginnings for their stories.

Audience: Yay! (cheers, etc.)

Guy: Thank you.

Ryan: High praise for Long Haired Rocker Guy! And now, our final contestant, Crissie Country!

Audience: (claps)

Crissie: Howdy, Everyone. Howdy, Ryan.

Ryan: You've got some tough competition tonight, Crissie. Are you ready?

Crissie: I'm ready! Woo-Hoo! I'm just a country girl in search of her destiny.

Ryan: Week to week you've been a consistent contestant. Let's see how you do tonight. Have you been working on your narrative beginning?

Crissie: Yes, I have.

Ryan: Take it away, Crissie Country!

...American Narrative Idol

Crissie: Okay. Here goes. (use weird voice) "Crisssss---sie!" It was the strangest voice I'd ever heard. I was walking home from school on a day that seemed like any other day, when the eerie voice called to me. Where was it coming from? I strained to listen."

Ryan: Let's show our support for Crissie Country!

Audience: (claps and cheers)

Ryan: Randy, what's the word?

Randy: Yo, Crissie. Good job, girl. You came out here and showed everyone that you know how to WRITE!!!!

Crissie: Thank you.

Ryan: Paula?

Paula: You're a winner, Crissie. Great job! You set up a scenario that made us want to keep reading. Well done!

Simon: Crissie, do you remember when I criticized you last week for using too many juicy color words?

Audience: Boo!

Simon: Well, I'm not going to do that this week. A million kids auditioned for this contest. Week by week we've narrowed down the competition until there are just a few of you left. Crissie, in my opinion, this was a fantastic example of a good narrative beginning. You might just end up in the finals.

Ryan: Crissie, high praise from Simon Growl and our other judges.

Crissie: Thank you. Hi to everyone watching back in Bug Holler!

Ryan: Well, that's it for tonight, Ladies and Gentlemen. YOU will be the judge of who stays....and who is voted off. Tune in tomorrow night to see the results. Our phone lines are open, so you can start voting...NOW! Simon, you were in rare form tonight, I might observe.

Simon: Oh, do shut up your obsessive twittering. You're giving me a headache.

Ryan: Somebody's in a bad mood.

Randy: Yo, Paula. What was the pirate movie rated?

Paula: I give up. What WAS the pirate movie rated?

Randy: (pirate voice) Ahrrrrrr!

Simon: That's it. I'm out of here. Does anyone have an aspirin?

Dr. Zee and the Museum of Ancient Curiosities

A Ten-Minute Play by Melissa Forney

Characters:

Dr. Eldermyer Zuckerman	Class (audience)
Teacher	Henry
Elvin	Demontez
Jodi	Kiera
Anna	Hunter

Setting: The Museum of Ancient Curiosities, the year 3009

Dr. Zee: Welcome, welcome, one and all ! I extend to you a heartfelt greeting of the utmost eagerness. Allow me to introduce myself. I'm Dr. Eldermyer Zuckerman, curator of the place in which you are now standing, the Museum of Ancient Curiosities. And I believe you are 4th grade students?

Teacher: Yes, Dr. Zuckerman, I'm Alice Cranberry, and this is my class of 4th graders from Thurston Howell Elementary. Thank you for agreeing to give us a personal tour of the museum. Class, please say hello to Dr. Zuckerman.

Class: Hello, Dr. Zuckerman.

Dr. Zee: Oh, please call me Dr. Zee. Everyone does. It's much easier to remember. Well, again, welcome Miss Cranberry. Hello there, kids. I'm delighted you're here. The Museum of Ancient Curiosities is a valuable collection of historic artifacts that teach us about mankind's progress through the centuries. Today we'll start our tour with the beginning of the 21st Century.

Henry: Yikes! That's over a thousand years ago.

Anna: Yeah. In class we had a study project about life in the year 2009. Kids played something called video games. They didn't have personal cyber companions, and they had to make their beds. Can you imagine? They didn't have virtual beds with laser-controlled thermal systems. How primitive! Ancient, man.

Elvin: And I saw some copies of People Magazine from 2009 on Antiques Roadshow. One copy was worth $12,000! They showed a few pages. The people in 2009 were all about clothes, movie stars, plastic surgery, beauty, and...being THIN.

Dr. Zee: Yes, life was certainly interesting back then. I received my doctorate degree in 21st century studies, and I'm frequently amazed by what people's priorities were. Since you've recently studied the early 21st century, let's start our tour with the year 2009. Follow me. (pause) Yes, here we are. Come closer so you can see. Gather round. (pause) Now, can anyone tell me what we're looking at?

Demontez: Uh...I think they called it....a washing machine? I saw it on the History Channel on SkyVision. They said people used to wash their clothes in it....at HOME!

Class: (Wow! Awesome! You're kidding! At home? etc.)

Kiera: They washed their clothes AT HOME? (pause) In THAT?

Dr. Zee: Exactly. In the year 2009 they hadn't invented soil removal stations. People sorted their clothing into darks, whites, sheets and towels, and put each load into the top of this machine. For the 21st century, this was an innovation.

...Dr. Zee

Demontez: How did it work?

Dr. Zee: You measured liquid or powdered soap and poured it over the clothes. The machine filled with water and then agitated the clothes, rinsed them, and spun out most of the moisture. It made quite a racket, actually, but it worked well.

Hunter: Liquid soap? Powdered soap? What about POWER 9000?

Dr. Zee: (laughs) Back then, POWER 9000 hadn't been invented yet. People also had to put their wet, washed clothing in a spin dryer and then fold them by hand.

Anna: Our clean clothes arrive every morning from the soil removal station folded and ready to wear. I can't imagine washing our clothes at home!

Dr. Zee: Let's move on to the next display.

Jodi: Whoa! What is that? It's gigantosaurus!

Dr. Zee: Can anyone guess?

Elvin: Some sort of...primitive...housing? Is that what they called a...trailer?

Hunter: Yeah! A trailer. I bet that's it. I've heard of a trailer.

Dr. Zee: Good guess, but no. Anyone else?

Demontez: Let's see...there are wheels...could it be...a portable cave?

Dr. Zee: Not a cave, but...a school bus. This is how some kids in the year 2009 traveled to school every morning.

Class: (Wow! A school bus? Look at that! How did it work? etc.)

Jodi: (shocked) You mean they didn't have their own personal propulsion pack?

Dr. Zee: No, 3P's hadn't been invented yet. Kids in the 21st century waited for this early transportation system to arrive in their neighborhoods. They boarded the school bus by this door and walked down the aisle to find a seat. A driver drove them, and sometimes it took as much as 45 minutes to arrive at school.

Henry: (shocked) 45 minutes? When I'm ready for school I just strap on my 3P60-20, press the button on the jet pack, hold on, and I'm there in 23 seconds!

Dr. Zee: I'm sure you remember to wear your helmet and face shield.

Henry: I do now. Once I forgot, and when I got to school I had a hummingbird stuck in my teeth.

Class: (everyone laughs)

Teacher: I don't think any of us will forget that day, Henry. It took me an hour to settle everyone down from laughing.

Dr. Zee: Ah! Here's something you'll want to see.

...Dr. Zee

Anna: What is it? It looks like some sort of writing. Didn't ancient civilizations use paper instead of uplinked telepads?

Dr. Zee: You know your history, Anna. They did indeed use paper. And what you're looking at is some writing written by a 4th grade class from the year 2009. I believe these were narrative stories.

Jodi: Gosh! They were the same age as us! And we learn narrative writing, too.

Kiera: Did they write the same way we do today, Dr. Zee?

Dr. Zee: Basically, yes. Kids in the 21st century wrote about things they liked, things they were interested in. But there are some subtle differences. Notice their use of immature transitional words: first, next, then, secondly, and finally.

Demontez: Wow. That sounds like kindergarten writing. First, next, then, finally...didn't they know about transitional *phrases* and *sentences?*

Dr. Zee: That's a good question. My research leads me to believe that they *did know* about transitional phrases and sentences...but they didn't always use them.

Hunter: Didn't they know that good transitions would make their writing much better?

Elvin: And more mature?

Dr. Zee: It could have been that they were a little lazy when it came to writing. Remember that the early 21st century was all about technology and gadgets. Some kids didn't have a strong work ethic.

Elvin: What's a work ethic?

Anna: It means they might not have wanted to make the effort to use really great transitions. Good writing takes work. I guess some kids wanted to do just enough to get by.

Hunter: Or maybe they got stuck in a rut and used the same old boring words over and over. Look at this sample. Almost every sentence starts with "next."

Jodi: Too bad. What a bore. Man, if I had my uplink pad with me I'd show that kid a thing or two about writing.

Dr. Zee: I like your thought process, Jodi. If it were possible to go back in a time machine and give some advice to the kids of the early 21st century, what would you tell them about their writing?

Jodi: That would be cool! First of all, I'd tell them that simple transitional words are not worthy of 4th grade writing. Then I'd give them a list of terrific transitional phrases and sentences.

Dr. Zee: For instance?

Jodi: Well, here's a few I've used recently: *later on that afternoon, wait till you hear what happened next, listen to this, the next step is not as easy as you'd think, when we got to the music room...*

...Dr. Zee

Teacher: Great job, Jodi. You're one of our strongest writers.

Dr. Zee: Superb transitional phrases and sentences, Jodi. The kids from the 21st century would do well to follow your advice. What else would you tell kids about their writing if you could travel back in time in a time machine?

Elvin: I'd tell them to support with reasons and details their readers can picture. Man, I'm telling you, greatness is in the details!

Henry: I'd tell them to include a mini-story. I do that every time and my writing is off the chain!

Kiera: Too bad we don't have a time machine!

Dr. Zee: Eh? Who says we don't have a time machine, Kiera?

Hunter: Are you saying you have a time machine?

Elvin: That actually works?

Dr. Zee: Well, I can see you've kept the secret, Miss Cranberry.

Teacher: Only their parents know, Dr. Zee. I have all the permission slips right here.

Anna: Secret? What secret, Dr. Zee?

Dr. Zee: Well, the truth of the matter is, students, that our institute actually *does* have a time machine. And you kids have been chosen to do just what we've been talking about. We're going back in time, almost a thousand years, so you can meet the kids of the 21st century and tell them what you've learned about writing. We'll only be gone for two hours. Are you ready for an adventure?

Kiera: Awesome! And our parents know about it?

Teacher: Yes, indeed. This trip in the time machine is our field trip. I've been keeping it a secret until I knew Dr. Zee could work out all the details for us to go.

Dr. Zee: We take groups of children back in time every single week day.

Demontez: My friends are not going to believe this! Let's get this party started!

Elvin: Radical! I've got my uplink telepad with me so I can record everything.

Jodi: This is going to be the best field trip ever!

Henry: I'm going to take my 3P60-20! Wait till they see me fly!

Dr. Zee: Step aboard. Take a seat around the sides. That's it. Make room for everyone. I've set the computerized teleport selector for the year 2009. Fasten your seatbelts. It takes just five seconds to stream. We'll be back in no time.

Hunter: Kids of 2009, ready or not, here we come!

Everyone: Five, Four, Three, Two, One.....BLASTOFF!

Paper Bag Writing Folder

Writers are innovative. This idea can help keep your writing organized all year long. Make it yourself with two paper bags.

Instructions for Making a Paper Bag Writing Folder

For this project you'll need:

scissors
wide transparent tape
one 18 inch piece of string

one drinking straw from McDonald's
cap pencil eraser
two large paper grocery bags

three sticky-back velcro dot sets
new pencil, sharpened
hole punch

1. Place the two brown paper bags side by side so that the smooth side (front) of the bags is facing up. The sides of the bags that have flaps will be facing down.

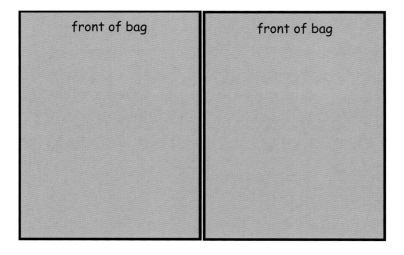

2. Get someone to help you hold the bags together side-by-side. Pull out a long piece of tape, longer than the length of the bags. Smooth the tape down over the seam of the two bags, and leave an eight inch "tail" of tape hanging down from the bottom.

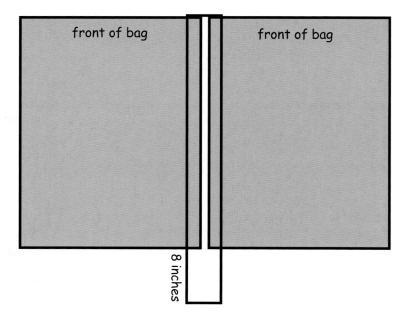

...Paper Bag Writing Folder

3. Flip the bags over and smooth the center tape up over the center seam and to the inside of the flap. Cut strips of tape for the sides flaps. Cover both side flap openings so they are taped shut. This forms a pouch for your pencils, medallions, paperclips, stickers, racing car, etc.

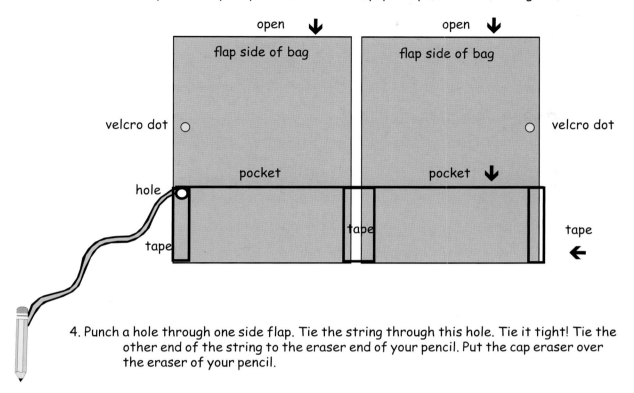

4. Punch a hole through one side flap. Tie the string through this hole. Tie it tight! Tie the other end of the string to the eraser end of your pencil. Put the cap eraser over the eraser of your pencil.

5. Cut off two inches of the plastic straw. Use this to cover your sharpened pencil. Take it off when you're writing. Put it back on to protect the pencil point when you are not writing. Your pencil point will last much longer.

6. Stick one velcro dot set near the inside edge so you can open and close your folder.

7. Stick one velcro dot set to the inside top of each bag so you can open and close each one, and things won't fall out.

8. Decorate the front of your writing folder so that it is uniquely yours. Go wild! Use photos, clip art, cool fonts, colored markers, stickers, sequins, etc.

9. Inside one of the folder bags, store unused writing paper. This will be handy for whenever you need to write. You can store different colors, sizes, and kinds of paper for projects you are working on.

10. Inside the other folder bag, store writing pieces you have completed, pieces you are still working on, your picture file, handouts, notes, correspondence, etc.

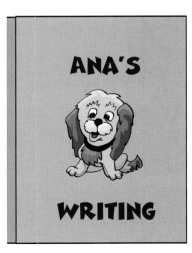

Answer Keys

Word Terms Word Search Page 60

audience
beginning
brainstorming
clues
conclusion
creativity
details
ending
expository
FCAT
Florida Writes
grabber
imagination
middle
narrative
partner
prompt
reader
takeaway ending
writer

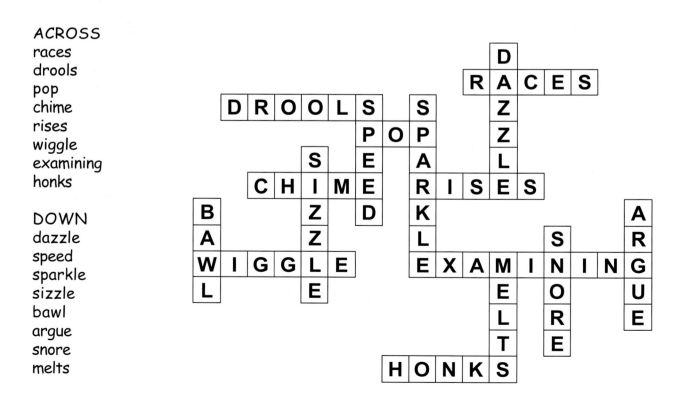

Strong Verb Crossword Page 103

ACROSS
races
drools
pop
chime
rises
wiggle
examining
honks

DOWN
dazzle
speed
sparkle
sizzle
bawl
argue
snore
melts

...Answer Keys

Conventions Crossword Page 128

ACROSS
1. subject
4. singular
6. first
9. exclamation point
12. apostrophe
13. agree
14. period
15. proper

DOWN
2. capital letter
3. present
5. question mark
7. capital letter
8. indent
10. double
11. commas

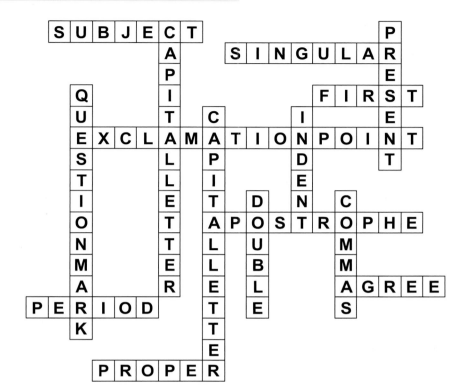

Sizzling Spelling Word Search Page 145

accident
amazed
beautiful
billionaire
choreography
disrespect
handicapped
gladiator
embarrass
famous
gigantic
gargantuan
imagination
knowledge
magical
monstrous
xylophone
Wednesday
vegetable
quickly
question
Florida

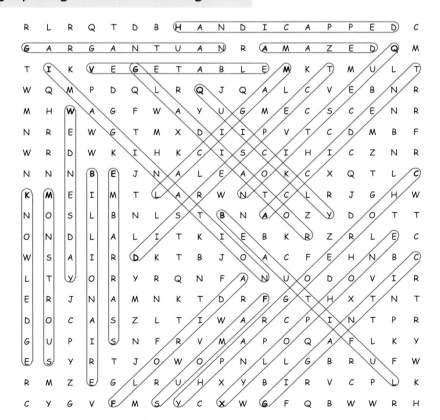

Bill Grogan's Goat Tune

Bill Grogan's Goat is sung as an echo song. One group sings the melody in the top line, and the other group echos on the second line. Have fun singing these silly words!

Lyrics by Melissa Forney

Arr. by P. Rossi

2

He took him to
The nearest school
And said, "This goat
Is not a fool!
Your kids should see
How well he writes
His dialogue
Is dynamite!"

3

"He uses 'voice'
With perfect ease
Transition words?
For him a breeze!
His sizzling verbs
Are filled with bliss
Can 4th grade kids
Write verbs like this?"

4

The teacher said,
"With your permission
I'd like to stage
A competition
We will go by
A judge's vote
My 4th grade kids
Against your goat!"

5

Bill Grogan clapped,
The children danced
The genius goat
Got up and pranced
He strutted 'round
And puffed his chest
And said, "You'll see
That I write best!"

6

But as they start-ed
With their caper
And kids took out
Their stacks of paper
The goat began
To chomp and munch
Until he'd eat-en
Up the bunch

7

He said, "This pa-per
I adore!
Please tell me that
There's much, much more!"
He ate it all
Yes, every sheet
Then burped real loud
And gave a bleet

8

The children laughed
With such delight
And said, "Who cares
If goats can write?
Can you believe
This great surprise?
He's eaten all
Our school supplies!"

9

And so they ne-ver
Really knew
If goats can write
But, hey, it's true
Some goats can write
So very fine
Instead of six
They get a nine

Writing Research

Applebee, Arthur N. and Judith A. Langer. (2006). "The State of Writing Instruction in America's Schools: What Existing Data Tells Us." Center on English Learning & Achievement.

Archer, Anita L. "A Model for Teaching Struggling Writers." http://www.ode.state.or.us/teachlearn/subjects/elarts/reading/literacy/summerinstitute/presentres/modelteachstrugglingwriters.pdf.

Baker, Scott, Russell Gersten and Steve Graham. (2003). "Teaching Expressive Writing to Students with Learning Disabilities: Research-based Applications and Examples." Journal of Learning Disabilities 36.2: 109-123.

Calkins, Lucy. (1993). *The Art of Teaching Writing*. Portsmouth: Heinemann.

Carbo, Marie. (2007). *Becoming a Great Teacher of Reading: Achieving High Rapid Reading Gains with Powerful, Differentiated Strategies*. Thousand Oaks: Corwin Press.

Carbo, Marie. (1997). *What Every Principal Should Know About Teaching Reading: How to Raise Test Scores and Nurture a Love of Reading*. Syosset: National Reading Styles Institute.

Claggett, Fran. "Teaching Writing: Craft, Art, Genre." NTCE Article 120802.

Collerson, J. (1988). *Writing for Life*. Newtown, NSW: Primary English Teaching Association.

Davis, Judy and Sharon Hill. (2003). *The No-Nonsense Guide to Teaching Writing: Strategies, Structures, and Solutions*. Portsmouth: Heinemann.

Dyson, Anne Haas. (1988). "Negotiating Among Multiple Worlds: The Space/Time Dimensions of Young Children's Composing." National Center for the Study of Writing, Technical Report No. 15.

Dyson, Anne Haas. (1987). "Unintentional Helping in the Primary Grades: Writing in the Children's World." National Center for the Study of Writing, Technical Report No. 2.

"Early Child Care Linked to Increases in Vocabulary." (2007). National Institutes of Health News.

Fauntas, Irene and Gay Sue Pinnell. (2001). *Guiding Readers and Writers, Grades 3-6: Teaching Comprehension, Genre, and Content Literacy*. Portsmouth: Heinemann.

Fletcher, Ralph. (2006). *Boy Writers: Reclaiming Their Voices*. Portland: Stenhouse.

Fletcher, Ralph and JoAnne Portalupi. (2007). *Craft Lessons: Teaching Writing K-8*. Portland: Stenhouse.

Freeman, Marcia. (1998). *Teaching the Youngest Writers*. Gainesville: Maupin House.

Gardner, Howard. (1993). *Multiple Intelligences: The Theory in Practice*. New York: Basic.

Gardner, Howard. (2000). *Intelligence Reframed: Multiple Intelligences for the 21st Century*. New York: Basic.

Gentry, J. Richard and Jean Wallace Gillett. (1997). *Teaching Kids to Spell*. Portsmouth: Heinemann.

Graves, Donald H. (1991). *Building a Literate Classroom*. Portsmouth: Heinemann.

Graves, Donald H. (2005). *Inside Writing: How to Teach the Details of Craft*. Portsmouth: Heinemann.

Herrmann, Andrea. "Teaching Writing with Peer Response Groups Encouraging Revision." (ERIC Clearinghouse on Reading, English, and Communication Digest #38).

Hornick, Karen. (2000). "Teaching Writing to Linguistically Diverse Students." ERIC Digest, Article ED275792.

Hudson, Richard. "Grammar Teaching and Writing Skills: The Research Evidence." Department of Phonetics and Linguistics, UCL, London.

"Improving the Reading Achievement of America's Children: 10 Research-Based Principles." (1998). CIERA.

Kurland, Daniel. (2000). "Learning to Read and Write." www.criticalreading.com.

Kurland, Daniel. (2000). "A Grammar for Reading and Writing." www.criticalreading.com.

Kurland, Daniel. (2000). "The Need to Improve Your Writing." www.criticalreading.com.

...Writing Research

Kurland, Daniel (2003). "The Spoken Word: The Base for Writing and Reading." www.criticalreading.com.

Lance, Wayne D. (2005). "Teaching Writing: The Elementary Years." International Children's Education. www.iched.org.

Manning, Maryann. (1987). *Reading and Writing in the Primary Grades*. Washington, D.C. : National Education Association.

McCormick, Kathleen. (1989). "Expanding the Repertoire: An Anthology of Practical Approaches for the Teaching of Writing." National Center for the Study of Writing. Technical Report No. 30.

Miller, Cathy Puett. "The Face of Effective Vocabulary Instruction." Education World: *Reading Coach*.

Montague, Nicole. (1995). "The Process Oriented Approach to Teaching Writing to Second Language Learners." New York State Association for Bilingual Education Journal, 13-24.

Nagin, Carl. (2003). *Because Writing Matters: Improving Writing in Our Schools*. Berkeley: National Writing Project.

"NCTE Beliefs about the Teaching of Writing." NCTC, Article

Nunley, Kathie F. (2004). "Active Research Leads to Active Classrooms." Dr. Kathie F. Nunley's Web Site. www.help4teachers.com.

Nunley, Kathie F. (2004). "Working With Styles." Dr. Kathie Nunley's Web Site for Educators. www.help4teachers.com.

Nunley, Kathie F. (2004). "Rubrics." Dr. Kathie Nunley's Web Site for Educators. www.help4teachers.com.

Pan, Barbara Alexander. (2007-2010). Research Project. "Validating Measures for Tracking Vocabulary Development of English Language Learners." U.S. Dept. of Health and Human Services, Administration for Children and Families.

"Priority: Literacy Best Practices." (2004). National Deaf Education Center. Gallaudet University.

Ray, Katie Wood. (1999). *Wondrous Words: Writers and Writing in the Elementary Classroom*. Urbana: NCTE.

Rosenshine, Barak. (1996). "Advances in Research on Instruction." Issues in Educating Students With Disabilities. Mahwah, 197-221.

Russell, Gersten, Scott Baker and Lana Edwards. (1999). "Teaching Expressing Writing to Students with Learning Disabilities." LD Online. www.ldonline.org.

Silberman, Arlene. (1989). *Growing Up Writing: Teaching Children to Write, Think, and Learn*. New York: Times Books.

Stead, Tony. (2003). *Is That a Fact: Teaching Non-Fiction Writing K-3*. Portsmouth: Stenhouse.

Stein, Victoria. (1989). "Elaboration: Using What You Know." National Center for the Study of Writing, Reading-to-Write. Report No. 6.

Stone, Sandra. (1994). "Strategies for Teaching Children in Multiage Classrooms." Childhood Education, Vol. 71.0

Strickland, Dorothy. (1989). *Emerging Literacy: Young Children Learn to Read and Write*. Newark: International Reading Association.

Strickland, Dorothy. (2004). *Learning About Print in Preschool: Working with Letters, Words, and Beginning Links with Phonemic Awareness*. Newark: International Reading Association.

Tobias, Cynthia. (1997). *Bringing Out the Best in Your Child : 80 Ways to Focus on Every Kid's Strengths*. Ann Arbor: Vine.

Tobias, Cynthia. (1999). *You Can't Make Me (But I Can Be Persuaded)*. Colorado Springs: Waterbrook Press.

Tobias, Cynthia. (2004). *I Hate School: How to Help Your Child Love Learning*. Grand Rapids, Zondervan.

"What Does Scientifically-Based Research Tell Us About Vocabulary Instruction?" National Institute for Literacy.

"Why Do Children Experience a Vocabulary Explosion at 18 Months of Age?" (2007). Science Daily.

Wray, David and Maureen Lewis. "Scaffolding Children's Writing in a Range of Genres." Exeter: University of Exeter.

"Writing in the Early Grades, K-2." NTCE, Article 113328.

"Writing in the Intermediate Grades, 3-5." NTCE, Article 115617.

Index

"as" similes 84
"like" similes 84
alligator score chart 182-183
answer keys 210-211
apostrophes 117
audience 25
beginning 17, 33-34, 40, 58-59
beginning, middle, ending paper 61
board game questions 132-140
brainstorming 29-32
capital letters 120-121
clues 49
crafts
    Terrific Table Tents 58-59
    Beginning, Middle, Ending Paper 61
    Magnetic Panorama 62
    Creativity Slider 110-112
    Writing Weight Chart 154-155
    Alligator Score Chart 182-183
    Score Tower 184-185
    Medallions 186-187
    Paper Bag Writing Folder 208
commas 119-120
commas in a series 120
comparisons 95
completeness 78
conclusion 49
conclusion practice 50-51
content 153
conventions 17, 128, 153
conventions crossword 128
creativity 153
creativity skills list 81
creativity slider 110-112
details 27, 44-45
details sample 45
dialogue 42, 91-92
double negatives 117
editing 113, 114
editing example 114
ending 17, 33-34, 58-59
exclamation point 120
explain 59
explaining 27
expository 59
expository beginnings 38-39
expository clues 27-28
expository example 34
expository five example 161
expository four example 160
expository prompt 31, 33
expository six example 162-163
expository storyboard questions 70-71
expository topics 20
expository writing sample 180-181
first person 116
Florida Writes 57
Florida Writes questions 15-16
Florida Writes scorers 17
Florida Writes scoring rubric 186
focus 17, 186
format 57
games
    Writing Skills Bingo 21
    Writing Terms Word Search 60
    Strong Verb Crossword 103
    Treasure Hunt Vocabulary Game 109
    Conventions Crossword 128
    Survival Game 130-131
    Race to the Finish 142-143
    Dazzling Spelling Word Search 145
global statement 42
grabber 40-42
grabber practice 43
grammar 116-119
handwriting 115
humorous statement 42
idioms 86
indentation 120
jotting 73
like-details 47-48
magnetic panorama 62
main idea 17
metaphors 85-86
middle 17, 33-34, 44, 58-59
"mind movie" 19, 44
mystery 42
narrative 59
narrative beginnings 36-37
narrative clues 26, 28
narrative example 35
narrative five example 157
narrative four example 156
narrative prompt 29
narrative six example 158-159
narrative storyboard questions 68-69
narrative topics 20
narrative writing sample 178-179

off topic 46
onomatopoeia 42, 104
opinion 42
organization 17, 57, 208
paper bag writing folder 208-209
partners 22-23
passion 105
periods 120
plays
   So You Think You Can Grab 192
   Writing Precinct 194
   Survivor: Expository Island 197
   American Narrative Idol 200
   Dr. Zee and the Museum of
      Ancient Curiosities 204
present tense verbs 118
punctuation 116-127
punctuation marks 120
punctuation practice 125-127
question mark 120
quotation marks 120
race to the finish game 141-143
reading a prompt 24
reasons and details 27, 97-99
revision 79-80
rhetorical question 42
run-on sentence 124
S.W.A.T. 96
scenario 42
score sheet 176
score tower 184-185
scorers 25
scoring 164-176
scoring writing samples 166-175
sentence combining 76-77
sentence fragments 122-123
sentence variety 74-75
similes 83-84
singular pronouns 116
sizzling vocabulary 108-109
sizzling vocabulary game 109
songs
   We're Going to Write Like
     Maniacs Tonight! 188
   A Kid Named Ted 188
   Adding the Writing Skills
     That You Have Learned 189
   Florida Writes! 189
   All for Florida Writes! 190

   At Least a Four and Maybe More 190
   Bill Grogan's Goat 191, 212
   The Boot Camp Song 191
specific emotion words 87-88
specific sensory words 89-90
specific statement 42
spelling 72, 144-152
spelling list 146-152
spelling word search 145
storyboarding 63-67
strong verb list 102
strong verbs 100-103
strong verbs crosswords 103
style 82
subject 118-119
subject/verb agreement 118
support 17
survival skill game 129-131
table tents 58
tacky expressions 96
takeaway endings 52-56
telling a story 59
temporary spelling 72
things to write 18-19
third person 116
time budgeting 177
transitional phrases 48, 93-94
transitional words 48
treasure hunt game 109
unnecessary details 46
verbs 119
vivid details 27
voice 42, 105-107
"word picture" 18-19, 100
word search 60
writing medallions 186-187
writing prompt 19
writing skills bingo 21
writing terms 60
writing with weight 154-155
writing research 213-214
writing samples
   narrative 35, 53-54, 56, 80, 93
   99, 101, 107, 114, 127, 156-159,
   166-167, 172-173, 178-179
writing samples
   expository 34, 45, 47- 48, 55, 98,
   106, 127, 160-163, 168-169,
   170-171, 174-175, 180-181

Now Including the Writing Superstars
Full Color CD so you Can Print Graphics, Games,
Crafts, Medallions, and Manipulatives
Easily from your Own Computer and Printer!

www.melissaforney.com
800-500-8176

Each CD Contains PDFs for:
Writing Skills BINGO
Table Tents
Writing Terms Word Search
Blank Storyboard
"As Similes"
"Like Similes"
Metaphors and Idioms
Transitional Phrase List
Strong Verb Crossword
Treasure Hunt Vocabulary Game
Creativity Slider
Grammar and Punctuation Rules

Seven "Superstar" Punctuation Marks
When to Use Capital Letters
Conventions Crossword
Survival Skill Game
Race to the Finish Game
Dazzling Spelling Word Search
A Spelling List for Genius Writers
Weight Lifting Sheet
Alligator Score Chart
Score Tower
Writing Medallions
Songs for Genius Writers
Bill Grogan's Goat Tune

Order Melissa Forney's Books

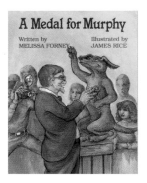

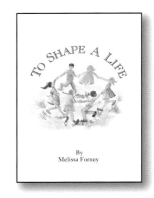

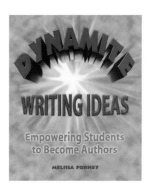

www.melissaforney.com
800-500-8176

Author, teacher, educational writing consultant Melissa Forney holds a Masters of Fine Arts in Writing for Children from Vermont College. Her dynamic **writing seminars, young authors conferences,** and humorous, motivational **keynote speeches** have delighted audiences for 14 years. She is a popular speaker and trainer at state, regional, national, and international educational conferences.

Schools using her writing books and training have achieved the highest writing assessment scores, revolutionized teaching strategies, and produced innovative, creative student writers. Her hands-on, energetic, teacher training and writing workshops consistently receive the highest evaluations.

An Excerpt from Melissa Forney's
Newest Historical Adventure Book

THE ASTONISHING JOURNEY OF TEDDY BODAIN

April 14, 1892

Dear Martha,

We crossed the river today. I sat on the bank again with Minnie, Hallie, Jasper, and Travis, only today I had Dylan with me. I had to watch him so Mama could help make sure all our things on the wagon stayed tied down and weren't damaged. After our wagon was locked in place on the ferry, Pap swam Jeb and January across the river. I was so proud. They swam over as pretty as you please and scrambled up the bank. Mama stayed with the wagon as it crossed on the ferry.

Minnie and Hallie held Veronica for me so Dylan wouldn't ruin her or get her dirty. I wasn't about to leave her on the wagon. Captain Walsh said that once in a while the ferry might tip over if the load wasn't balanced just right and our belongings would all be swept down river.

While we were sitting on the bank, Travis said, "Whose doll is that?" and pointed at Veronica.

I said, "Mine."

He said, "How did her hair get so real-looking?"

I told him about how your mother used cuttings of your real hair to make Veronica's hair.

He said, "Oh, Jasper, will you cut my hair so I can glue it on some dumb doll?"

I said, "Hush up, Travis."

And of course he said, "Hush up, Travis" in a girl's voice.

He said, "And we can dress her in frilly clothes and have a tea party."

I said, "Just remember that I whipped you in the slingshot competition."

He said, "I taught you everything you know!"

I said, "I'm not sharing any more of my jerky with you!"

Before I could realize what was happening, Travis snatched Veronica from Hallie and ran down to the river. He held her over the water and said, "How would you like it if I dropped your precious Veronica in this river?"

I screamed, "Stop! No!" I reached for her. Travis tried to hold her up over his head but she flew out of his hand and sailed into the river.

We both had the most astonished looks on our faces. I was furious! I screamed, "My baby! She's in the river!"

Travis was in a panic. He screamed, "Jasper, help! I dropped her in the river." He dived in and began searching. When he came up for air, he screamed at Jasper again, "Help me!" He knew he had done something terrible.

I stood there frozen to the spot. I heard some adults shouting. Folks came running from all directions. I heard Mama scream. I turned my head just in time to see her jump off the ferry into the water. She swam like her life depended on it. I thought, what on earth is she doing?

Captain Walsh shouted, "You men! Come help here!"

Mama staggered through the shallower water, her arms reaching out. She screamed, "Where is he? Where is he?" I had no idea what she was talking about. She looked more frightened than I had ever seen. She screamed, "Where is my baby? Where is my baby?"

I yelled, "Mama, Dylan's right here with Minnie. Travis threw Veronica in the river!"

Mama's face changed immediately. She found Dylan with her eyes, sitting on Minnie's lap. She glared at me. "What were you screaming about? I thought the baby had drowned!" Mama burst into tears.

I said, "Travis threw Veronica in the river."

Everyone standing there looked over at Travis. He had Veronica in his hands. She was dripping wet and most of her hair had come off.

Today was not a good day.

Love,

Teddy